Learning the Ropes:
Insights for Political
Appointees

IBM Center for
The Business
of Government

THE IBM CENTER FOR THE BUSINESS
OF GOVERNMENT BOOK SERIES

SERIES EDITORS: MARK A. ABRAMSON AND PAUL R. LAWRENCE

The IBM Center Series on The Business of Government explores new approaches to improving the effectiveness of government at the federal, state, and local levels. The Series is aimed at providing cutting-edge knowledge to government leaders, academics, and students about the management of government in the 21st century.

Publications in the series include:

Collaboration: Using Networks and Partnerships, *edited by John M. Kamensky and Thomas J. Burlin*
E-Government 2003, *edited by Mark A. Abramson and Therese L. Morin*
E-Government 2001, *edited by Mark A. Abramson and Grady E. Means*
Human Capital 2004, *edited by Jonathan D. Breul and Nicole Willenz Gardner*
Human Capital 2002, *edited by Mark A. Abramson and Nicole Willenz Gardner*
Innovation, *edited by Mark A. Abramson and Ian D. Littman*
Leaders, *edited by Mark A. Abramson and Kevin M. Bacon*
Managing for Results 2005, *edited by John M. Kamensky and Albert Morales*
Managing for Results 2002, *edited by Mark A. Abramson and John M. Kamensky*
Memos to the President: Management Advice from the Nation's Top Public Administrators, *edited by Mark A. Abramson*
New Ways of Doing Business, *edited by Mark A. Abramson and Ann M. Kieffaber*
The Procurement Revolution, *edited by Mark A. Abramson and Roland S. Harris III*
Transforming Government Supply Chain Management, *edited by Jacques S. Gansler and Robert E. Luby, Jr.*
Transforming Organizations, *edited by Mark A. Abramson and Paul R. Lawrence*

Learning the Ropes: Insights for Political Appointees

EDITED BY

MARK A. ABRAMSON
IBM CENTER FOR THE BUSINESS OF GOVERNMENT
and
PAUL R. LAWRENCE
IBM BUSINESS CONSULTING SERVICES

ROWMAN & LITTLEFIELD PUBLISHERS, INC.
Lanham • Boulder • New York • Oxford

ROWMAN & LITTLEFIELD PUBLISHERS, INC.

Published in the United States of America
by Rowman & Littlefield Publishers, Inc.
A wholly owned subsidiary of The Rowman & Littlefield Publishing Group, Inc.
4501 Forbes Boulevard, Suite 200, Lanham, Maryland 20706
www.rowmanlittlefield.com

PO Box 317
Oxford
OX2 9RU, UK

British Library Cataloguing in Publication Information Available

Library of Congress Cataloging-in-Publication Data

Learning the ropes : insights for political appointees / edited by Mark A. Abramson and
Paul R. Lawrence.
    p. cm.
Includes bibliographical references.
ISBN 0-7425-4985-2 (cloth : alk. paper) — ISBN 0-7425-4986-0 (pbk. : alk. paper)
1. Government executives—United States. 2. United States—Officials and employees.
3. Civil service—United States—Personnel management. I. Abramson, Mark A., 1947-
II. Lawrence, Paul R., 1956-
JK723.E9L436 2005
352.6'3'0973—dc22   2005007853

Printed in the United States of America

♾™ The paper used in this publication meets the minimum requirements of American
National Standard for Information Sciences—Permanence of Paper for Printed Library
Materials, ANSI/NISO Z39.48-1992.

To future leaders:

Dylan Louis Abramson

Allison Page Lawrence

Gregory James Lawrence

TABLE OF CONTENTS

CHAPTER ONE

The Biggest Secret in Washington

Mark A. Abramson
Executive Director
IBM Center for The Business of Government

Paul R. Lawrence
Partner, IBM Business Consulting Services
and
Partner-in-Charge
IBM Center for The Business of Government

Introduction

Over 25 years ago, Hugh Heclo wrote a book called *A Government of Strangers: Executive Politics in Washington*.[1] The book explored what Heclo called "the relatively unknown process by which high-ranking political executives and bureaucrats interact with each other in Washington." In describing the relationship, Heclo wrote, "… political executives typically arrive in office expecting to deal with 'Washington bureaucrats,' not people…. Signals indicating a lack of trust are readily apparent." Heclo concluded that the lack of an effective working relationship between political appointees and career civil servants often diminishes the performance of government.

Heclo ends his book with a series of structural recommendations, including the creation of a "Federal Service," aimed at improving this relationship. His proposed "Federal Service" resembles the Senior Executive Service (SES), which was created in 1978 (a year after the Heclo book was published) by the Civil Service Reform Act of that year. While the creation of the SES was, for the most part, a positive development in the evolution of the senior career civil service, there is widespread agreement that the reform has not fully lived up to its potential and has not significantly improved the relationship between political appointees and career civil servants.

So where are we today? Heclo's description of a "government of strangers" is still largely accurate. Each four years, a new group of political appointees arrives in Washington. The arrival of new appointees does not just occur at the start of an administration. It continues throughout the first term of a president as many political appointees experience "burn out" at the end of two years and either return to the private sector or accept another position within government. If a president has the opportunity to serve a second term (an opportunity experienced by only four of our last nine presidents), the turnover among political appointees in the second term is also considerable. Of the four presidents since 1960 who have started a second term, President George W. Bush has had the greatest turnover among cabinet secretaries.[2] That turnover has quickly filtered down to the sub-cabinet: deputy secretaries, agency heads, assistant secretaries, and their staffs.

In some instances, career civil servants do, in fact, know their new political appointees. With our tradition of "in and outers," many former political appointees return to government when their party returns to power (often in more senior positions). Career civil servants often have worked with their "new" political appointee in a prior administration. For instance, a small group of political appointees from the Jimmy Carter administration returned to government in the Clinton administration. The George W. Bush administration includes alumni from the Ford, Reagan, and George H. W. Bush administrations. In other cases, career civil servants might know the new political appointee from their professional community—for example,

---

How NOT to Create Good Working Relationships

Political appointees should not say:
"Now that I'm here, there's going to be a lot of changes in this place."

Career executives should not say:
"We don't do things that way around here."

---

lawyers know lawyers, and transportation professionals know other transportation professionals, throughout the nation. But, for the most part, the imagery of a "government of strangers" is still very accurate.

Additional structural "solutions" to this fact of life of American government are unlikely. The United States will probably not adopt a parliamentary system of government anytime soon, along the lines of the United Kingdom system of "shadow cabinets" and "career deputy ministers." Thus, we are likely to continue with the "government of strangers" syndrome.

So what is to be done? One "solution" is relatively easy and straightforward. That solution is to acknowledge and publicize the biggest "secret" in Washington:

Political appointees and career executives need one another; neither group can succeed without the other.

Their success is interdependent. There are few, if any, examples of organizations that have "succeeded" in accomplishing their mission without both "sides" working together as a team. Political appointees cannot achieve their organizational priorities and goals without the support of their career staff. There are simply too few political appointees to get it all done by themselves (even though many teams of political appointees try hard to do so). Conversely, career executives lack the authority and "clout" to achieve organizational objectives without the full support of their political appointees. While one might find examples of career executives succeeding in achieving organizational goals without the support of the political hierarchy, those examples are few and far between.

During the 1980s, a British television show—*Yes Minister*—aired on U.S. public television channels. The comedy series presented stories about the relationship between the political appointee/minister (Jim Hacker, MP) and his senior careerist/permanent secretary (Sir Humphrey Appleby) in the United Kingdom Department of Administrative Affairs. There are several interpretations that one could make of the series. Based on several episodes, one could conclude that Sir Humphrey excelled at manipulating

Minister Hacker and expanding his department's staff and budget, as well as his own power. But in other episodes, Minister Hacker successfully comes to the rescue of Sir Humphrey, whose attempts at bureaucratic aggrandizement often got him into trouble. A viewing of the entire series shows that Minister Hacker and Sir Humphrey developed a very close, interdependent relationship. Each needed the other—neither was powerful, influential, or smart enough alone to achieve his department's mission. The story of Minister Hacker and Sir Humphrey is repeated daily in federal office buildings throughout Washington. (In a sequel also shown in the United States, *Yes, Prime Minister*, Jim Hacker enters the fight for party leadership and becomes Prime Minister, and Sir Humphrey moves up the civil service hierarchy to become Cabinet Secretary. In the sequel, their interdependence continues as both find their mutual success closely linked to their working together.)

While Minister Hacker and Sir Humphrey showed the value of teamwork and partnership, the folklore of Washington is filled with stories of political appointees and career executives "at war" with each other. While such stories make for good gossip, the consequence of such "at war" situations is that those organizations will likely *not* succeed in accomplishing either their organization's mission or the goals of their president. The agencies that succeed are more often those in which political appointees have formed effective working relationships with career civil servants.

Washington folklore also abounds with stories in which career civil servants successfully implemented an administration's desire to "close down" or reorganize either their entire agency or programs within their agencies— actions clearly against their own parochial interests. But the untold story of Washington is that civil servants, with effective political leadership at the top, will and have supported the directions and initiatives of an administration elected by the nation, be it Republican or Democratic. Civil servants do know that their job is to support the elected president and carry out his policies and programs (within the existing law, of course). There have been instances where civil servants have felt uncomfortable with an administration; many of them made the correct decision to leave government and continue their careers in the nonprofit or private sector, or to find another federal organization in Washington where they might be more comfortable.

The Challenge of Defining Roles

The keys to creating successful, productive relationships between political appointees and career executives are straightforward:
* Mutual respect (as in any effective organization)
* An understanding that each has a different job

A common problem that frequently hampers the development of effective working relationships in government occurs when political appointees and career executives don't fully understand that each has a different job and role in our government. In chapter three, Joseph Ferrara and Lynn Ross provide a fascinating case study where a career civil servant found herself in "trouble" with her political appointees due to role confusion. In setting forth "rules of engagement," Ferrara and Ross begin an important discussion about the respective roles of political and career executives in government. Each has a different job, focus, and emphasis, with both serving the nation and the Constitution.

Additional research on respective roles would be highly useful in creating a better understanding among both political and career executives. For career executives, the following roles are crucial to the success of their organization:

- Serving the public trust through the career civil service.
- Providing "collegial" leadership among peers to develop a strong, shared vision of their organization's mission.
- Serving as guardians for the well-being of their organization.
- Providing "subordinate" leadership to political executives.
- Serving as a catalyst for ongoing program improvement within their organization.[3]

If career executives can successfully fulfill these roles, the performance of their organization is likely to flourish and the likelihood of a productive working relationship with their political appointees increases.

There are also specific roles and responsibilities that political appointees should undertake as well. These include:

- Serving the public trust through the implementation of the President's policies and priorities.
- Understanding, adding to, clarifying, and reinforcing the organization's vision.
- Leaving a stronger institution behind than they found.
- Communicating the social value of their organization to the public.
- Supporting career executives' quest for improving the performance of the organization.

The Challenge of Competing Factions

None of this is easy. Fulfilling each of the above roles clearly comes under the category "easier said than done." But the goal should be straightforward and easily understood: creating a team within the organization, with all working toward a shared vision. While the concepts of team, teamwork, and vision were in vogue as management buzzwords during the 1990s, the concepts are still worthwhile and are crucial in creating effective organizations. It is all too easy for government organizations to fall into factions, not working together and, even worse, working at cross-purposes.

Examples of such factions are numerous. The traditional "faction" has been "career versus political." But frequently other factions are at work as well within government organizations, although they have received less publicity and attention. One less known problem hindering the creation of successful organizations is "career versus career" factions. While it is frequently presumed that careerists are all on the "same side," this is sometimes not the case. As in many organizations, careerists have tangled with each other over turf, budgets, and personal allegiances. Sometimes these historical tangles are forgotten and individuals "move on" to the latest battle or issue. But sometimes the baggage of past battles lingers on and the organization suffers. It is often hard for political appointees to create "one team" within their organization when careerists are "fighting" each other.

Another faction is "political versus political." While some high-level political infighting (such as fights between a secretary of state and a secretary of defense) do get attention, it is all too often forgotten that the "politicals" often do not agree with each other and are engaged in their own turf and power struggles in Washington. If the political appointees are spending much of their time fighting each other, there is little time or energy left over to form partnerships and effective working relationships with their career staffs.

Often these political factions each have their own political agendas and political allegiances. Historically, cabinet secretaries and deputy secretaries have sometimes been appointed from different wings of their own parties, each representing a distinct faction. Occasionally they have formed effective working relationships, but many times they have not.

Often factions are clearly identifiable through geography. In the Kennedy administration, the Irish Massachusetts "mafia" was clearly known. In the Carter administration, the Georgia contingent stood out, as did the "non-Georgians." During the Reagan administration, there were identifiable "Northern California" and "Southern California" contingents—each of which did not fully agree or support each other. Today, many in government are aware whether or not their political appointee is from Texas.

Looking Ahead

As noted earlier, the George W. Bush administration now has the opportunity to become only the third administration in the last 45 years to complete a second term. Many of the appointees who have signed on to stay for the second term have indeed "learned the ropes" and in many cases now know how to work with career civil servants and engage them for maximum productivity. The remaining chapters in this book are aimed at new political appointees who have been selected to join the administration and accomplish the president's goals and objectives for his second term. The message of this book is clear: Creating productive partnerships with career civil servants is crucial to achieving those goals and objectives.

Endnotes

1. Hugh Heclo, *A Government of Strangers: Executive Politics in Washington* (Washington, D.C.: Brookings Institution, 1977).

2. At the start of his second term, President George W. Bush selected nine new cabinet members. Only six cabinet secretaries continued from the end of the first term: the Secretary of Defense, the Secretary of Treasury (who, in fact, replaced the previous Secretary at the end of the administration's first two years), the Secretary of Transportation, the Secretary of Labor, the Secretary of the Interior, and the Secretary of Housing and Urban Development (who was appointed in the third year of the Bush administration).

In 1984, President Ronald Reagan selected seven new cabinet secretaries (out of the then 14 cabinet departments.) In 1996, President Bill Clinton also selected seven new cabinet secretaries.

3. For a discussion of subordinate and collegial leadership, see Mark A. Abramson and John W. Scanlon, "The Five Dimensions of Leadership," *Government Executive*, July 1991.

PART I

Working with Career Executives

Becoming an Effective Political Executive: 7 Lessons from Experienced Appointees

Judith E. Michaels

This report was originally published in January 2001, with a second edition in January 2005.

Introduction*

Federal service in Washington, D.C., is a unique experience for which no other training can prepare you. Nevertheless, research offers clues about who will do well as appointees, who will enjoy their tenure in the nation's capital, and who will be less than successful. Analysis informs this chapter, which is offered as a tool for those considering or newly entered into life as a political appointee, in the hopes that you will not only survive but thrive. This chapter is based on studies of and interviews with Senate-confirmed presidential appointees (PASs) in the fourth year of George H. W. Bush's administration (1992) and in the fourth year of Bill Clinton's first administration (1996).†

The chapter is organized into the "7 Lessons from Experienced Appointees," each of which discusses specific aspects of appointee work, including relations with career staff and other political appointees, stress, and relations with the White House, the Congress, and the media. It employs survey results, discussion, and direct quotes from political appointees and long-time career executives.

Based on the insights gained from these political appointees and career executives, we arrived at the following "7 Lessons from Experienced Appointees":

1. Turn to Your Careerists
2. Partner with Your Political Colleagues
3. Remember the White House
4. Collaborate with Congress
5. Think Media
6. Pace Yourself
7. Enjoy the Job

Our hope is that you will use these lessons—and master these habits—to help ensure that your experience in Washington will produce a successful and valuable contribution to public service.

Good luck to you!

---

* The author would like to thank Michael DeMarco, IBM Business Consulting Services, for his assistance in the preparation of this chapter.
† Unless noted, all quotes are from the author's personal interviews with appointees. Quotes from the Bush appointees are from the author's The President's Call: Executive Leadership from FDR to George Bush, University of Pittsburgh Press, 1997.

7 Lessons from Experienced Appointees

1. Turn to Your Careerists

As a presidential appointee, you will learn to relate to a variety of federal employees across many agencies during your time in federal service. Success will come from having the flexibility to know whom to consult and when, and whose judgment to trust. Experience has shown that appointees have much to gain by leading and utilizing the career employees, who too often are labeled as over-protected, inertia-laden, 9-to-5ers whose loyalties presumably lie with the previous administration. More often, though, careerists are very supportive of their boss, accept leadership readily, and identify much more with their agency than with a political party. As a result, most appointees come to rely heavily on their careerists in every aspect of their work, both political and administrative. Many appointees speak of their trust in careerists and how much they depend on them for policy guidance, as well as how they have kept them informed about the culture of their agency.

Some 73 percent of the past appointees surveyed gave a very positive assessment of the competency of their careerists, while 65 percent applied the same assessment to careerists' responsiveness.

Table 2.1: To What Degree Do You Find Your Career Colleagues to Be Competent and Responsive to Policy Direction?

	Great and Very Great
Competent (N=343)	73%
Responsive (N=339)	65%

Clearly, careerists can be a great help to you throughout your stay in Washington's halls of power. Of course, knowing that the data overwhelmingly supports careerists is one thing; knowing how to utilize your careerists' expertise and, at the same time, understand and minimize the effects of those cultural attributes unique to Washington's career brigade is yet another.

"The assumption of every new political group coming in is that career civil servants are captives of the previous administration.... But the message to political appointees is that they are not going to get their jobs done if they don't work closely with the senior people—and that they shouldn't assume that they are the enemy within." (From John Trattner, The 2000 Prune Book: How to Succeed in Washington's Top Jobs [Washington: Brookings Institution Press, 2000], p. 23)

— *Anonymous*

"Appointees are so vulnerable, they can sabotage themselves with an attitude of forcing the careerists or ignoring them.... You should take the time to ... get their input and agreement. Build on credibility from past work, call in the experts and get their input... Be a consensus manager rather than a dictator."

— *Bill Clinton appointee*

"Get the Line People Behind You"

Proper care and feeding of the career staff should be high on appointees' "must do" list from day one. Career employees know how government works, the ins and outs of their agency, and—perhaps most important—how the image game in Washington works.

Perception is reality in the judgmental fishbowl that is political Washington, policed by the cynical and very public eye of the *Washington Post*. And because the rules are different in government, people coming from the private sector can blunder unwittingly and damage themselves by doing something completely acceptable in the business world, such as accepting a free lunch or golf weekend, that is unethical in government service.

A supportive careerist can save an appointee from a costly image and common sense mistake, such as redecorating their office in an agency suffering cutbacks. Of course, a careerist you haven't "cared for" might choose to simply sit and watch as an appointee thrashes about in a tempest of her or his own making. It's up to you to build that relationship from the start through interaction and respect.

But can careerists really be trusted to help you succeed? New appointees, especially new appointees after a party change, naturally will be suspicious of a potential conspiracy. However, our research shows that as a group, careerists want to help their bosses, in large part because they identify with their programs much more so than they identify with the political party of the incoming or outgoing administration. The key is to provide leadership, set a tone for your agency, and understand the way the city operates. For instance, appointees shouldn't take in-house games personally, they just go with the territory. As Bonnie R. Cohen, former under secretary for management in the Department of State and assistant secretary for policy, management and budget at the Department of Interior, said, "Staff do go around me to Congress, but I don't consider that sabotage; it's just the way Washington works."

An appointee does well to look to the knowledge and institutional memory of careerists and to assume going in that they want what is best for their agency and will support the politicals as long as they feel that they receive support in return. One Clinton appointee advised, "Establish a really good rapport with the careerists at the executive level (members of Senior Executive Service, or SES). Recruit a confidential assistant from the career rank within the agency. They will already know the agency, be loyal to you, and know both worlds."

Bonnie Cohen put it in a nutshell when she said, "First, don't undertake a witch hunt. Second, have great respect for the expertise of the career employees—there were 70,000 at Interior. Use them to inform your decisions. Third, get to know the staff on the Hill."

Cohen's advice sounds simple, but, of course, nothing is as easy as it seems. As with any professional niche, D.C.'s careerists have a culture that has evolved over time and that can frustrate and derail appointees who don't maintain perspective.

Leadership Is Needed

Rather than bemoan the problems inherent within the careerists' environment, appointees must immediately get to work to set a direction that compensates for the problems as much as reasonably possible. It's a matter of leadership. The fact is, careerists as a group are like people in any profession, with excellent, average, and poor performers populating each agency. Says one Clinton appointee: "I have found great allies and immovable objects in both camps, career and political … some are top notch, some very poor—it's all in the selection process." The effective appointees will find and best utilize the excellent and average careerists, placing them in the right roles.

Donald Laidlaw, former assistant secretary for human resources and administration in the Department of Education, spoke of the leadership role of the politicals: "Setting the right tone is key. Giving direction is the appointee's job. After all, when the boat misses the harbor it's seldom the harbor's fault. Have fun, establish relations with the career people. They look at us as the Christmas help. You need their support."

After having worked with them, appointees rated the career SESs highly. When asked for specifics, two-thirds to 91 percent of the PASs surveyed rated their career subordinates "generally" or "greatly" helpful in major aspects of their work, such as a mastery of policy, technical, and implementation details, liaison with the bureaucracy and with Congress, and day-to-day management.

Table 2.2: In Specific Areas, Do Your Career SES Colleagues Help or Hinder Your Work?

	Generally and Greatly Help	Help as Much as Hinder	Generally and Greatly Hinder
Technical analysis of difficult issues	91%	6%	3%
Handling day-to-day management tasks	87%	11%	2%
Mastering substantive policy details	87%	9%	4%
Liaison with the federal bureaucracy	83%	13%	4%
Anticipating potential policy implementation problems	80%	15%	5%
Liaison with Congress	68%	26%	7%

"Careerists have it as part of their culture to support the boss.... Their program identification is very high and they will tend to resist change there.... I have trusting relations with the careerists in the building. They keep me informed about what's going on."
— *Anthony McCann, former Assistant Secretary for Management and Budget, Department of Veterans Affairs*

"There's a danger of building a wall between yourself and the career staff; you can do damage to the agency if you shut them out. Rely on careerists. They helped me cement my relationship with the career staff, restored relationships, and healed scars left by the previous director, who had alienated careerists."
— *Appointee who served both the Bush and Clinton administrations*

"My goal is to empower careerists in policy making, make them stakeholders."
— *Deborah Wince-Smith, former Assistant Secretary, Technology Policy Office, Technology Administration, Department of Commerce*

"Motivation is very important for the mission of your agency. If you don't believe in it, if you don't believe it will make a difference in the lives of ordinary people, stop doing it. Go do something else. Because if you don't believe in it, it's going to show to everybody. Everybody will notice that you're there more for the ride than for the goal." (From Trattner, p. 51)

— Former White House official

"There is a lot of paranoia on both sides of the political/career divide. Government needs managers who can divide fact from fiction."

— Bill Clinton appointee

"They are a joy to work with. It's a pleasure to try to live up to them by trying my best to be a good leader for them. Most civil servants are here because they like doing the deals, they like the sense of completion, accomplishment."

— Martin Kamarck, former Chair,
Export-Import Bank of the United States

"Public servants are obvious targets—your tax dollars pay for them, so you feel you can rough them up. We can't afford the luxury of trashing public servants."

— Charles Baquet, former Deputy Director, Peace Corps

"You can't develop policy without dealing with careerists. On balance they're pretty good; there's a remarkable level of competence considering the level of protection they have."

— Roland R. Vautour, former Under Secretary for Small Community
and Rural Development, Department of Agriculture

"The competence of an appointee influences her or his willingness to ask questions, to seek the counsel of careerists. The more competent and self-confident, the more willing to ask questions and seek counsel. There are three areas where appointees trip up the most: their inability to deal with the Congress, the media, and interest groups."

— Constance Berry Newman, current Assistant Secretary,
Bureau of African Affairs, Department of State,
and former Director, Office of Personnel Management

2. Partner with Your Political Colleagues

Political appointees encompass a diversity of skill levels and "political smarts." As in any workplace, you will find some of your colleagues to be very good, while others leave something to be desired. As one Clinton appointee put it: "The good ones have strong interpersonal skills, take great pride in their work, have a good work ethic, people judgement, are consummate professionals and politically savvy. Either they come that way or they pick it up quickly, but they are not politically driven, they have a degree of trust, can work in a situation of give and take, are not excessively authoritarian, work in the pluralism and decentralism in a bureaucracy and know how to make it work. These characteristics come in any variety of people—men, women, gay, straight, black, white, military, civilian."

And, by and large, our respondents thought very highly of their peers and political SES colleagues, as shown in Tables 2.3 and 2.4. Appointees consider their colleagues generally to be very competent, and thus consult with them regularly on a wide variety of policy, budget, and personnel issues.

Table 2.3: To What Degree Do You Find Your Political Colleagues to Be Competent and Responsive to Policy Direction?

	Great and Very Great	Moderate	No, Little and Somewhat
PAS			
Competent	76%	17%	7%
Responsive	83%	12%	5%
Non-career SES			
Competent	73%	20%	7%
Responsive	83%	11%	6%

One George H. W. Bush appointee judged the quality of her political peers as good, attributing it partly to "the Senate confirmation that insures better quality. The non-confirmed political staff, on the other hand—the chiefs of staff and special assistants (non-career SES and Schedule C)—are the more troublesome. They are the right-hand person, the closest aide to the secretary, and they often try to push around and dominate the political structure. They operate ruthlessly with the careerists. They aren't in charge of any line operations; they serve their principal and carry personal loyalty only to that person."

In observing what makes an effective appointee, Charlie Grizzle, former assistant administrator for administration and resources management at the Environmental Protection Agency (EPA), notes, "The successful ones are open-minded, willing to learn, to trust, they possess a sixth sense of when to delegate and when to make a decision oneself, noting the fine line between responsibility and authority."

He feels that "too many appointees come in with an agenda—they want to accomplish one or two specific things. This is a fatal flaw—you have to deal with everything that's on your plate, you can't let everything else go in the name of your agenda. Your principal task is to manage the organization you inherit. Stewards/managers will have a more lasting impact than cause-oriented appointees. Generalists/political animals (those who understand the political process) will have more success than the apolitical/technical people, who don't have a feel for the political process or how the town or the country works."

Table 2.4: How Often Do You Consult With Your Political Colleagues?

	Very Often and Always	Often	Some and Seldom
PAS			
Policy feasibility	71%	17%	12%
Policy formulation and development	74%	14%	12%
Policy implementation	68%	16%	15%
Budget decisions	62%	16%	22%
Personnel decisions	47%	16%	37%
Non-career SES			
Policy feasibility	63%	19%	17%
Policy formulation and development	64%	18%	18%
Policy implementation	65%	16%	19%
Budget decisions	58%	18%	25%
Personnel decisions	47%	19%	34%

Martha A. Krebs, former director, Office of Energy Research at the Department of Energy, said, "The gulf between the assistant secretaries and the front office (the secretary) is pretty wide. The pressures on them are so extraordinary in terms of the president and the Congress. The front office staff (the undersecretary, the deputy secretary, and "the Palace Guard") finds working with the department staff is never as satisfying as getting the guidance from the top. Consequently, I don't get the feedback I need or get it as promptly as I need it. Most of the time, when we see them is when they have to knock our heads together. You don't get their engagement on a positive level, they don't have enough time to do enough of it." Krebs continued, "Being an assistant secretary has limitations on what you can do in an agency. The measure of the job is not the dollars. A cabinet agency is much more complex than I expected. It's hard to get your message up to the front office, harder to get up to them than to the general public. You have to work them the way you work the White House or Congress. Get outside people to support your programs."

As the late Elliot Richardson, who served as secretary in four departments, noted, agency heads' sole responsibility is for the issues under that agency. This makes them less willing to consult other heads, so they're isolated by virtue of the job. He quoted "Miles' Law" (set forth by Rufus Miles, a former senior careerist at the Department of Health, Education and Welfare): "'Where you stand depends on where you sit.' Subsequently, synergy and consistency of programmatic activities have to be lodged in the White House and decision making has to be done by the White House in terms of cabinet committees and issues because each cabinet member is autonomous and nothing can bind them to a plan except a White House decree. However, there's always been a lot of connection among the sub-cabinet officials."

Ed Timperlake, former assistant secretary for public affairs at the Department of Veterans Affairs, noted, "There is a sense of isolation within the agencies. Henry Kissinger was right when he said, 'The immediate drives out the important.'"

Because political appointee jobs are often the reward for campaign work, places have to be found for as many partisans as possible. Often supporters are given Schedule C positions, but there is a danger in over-using them. Carol A. Bonosaro, president of the Senior Executives Association, mentioned a cabinet secretary who surrounded himself with Schedule Cs. "Maybe it's because he wanted to get things done in a hurry, but it's like putting a moat around the secretary," she said.

Another reason not to rely too much on Schedule Cs was voiced by a Clinton appointee who said, "I prefer not to have Schedule Cs because of the uncertainties of who will choose them and what their agenda is, who they're loyal to, what their skills are."

"If the secretary leaves, there is a revolution within the agency. Cabinet government is dictatorship. The departure of the secretary ends the agenda within the agency. It's life and death for the appointees in the agency. It's less of a problem when lower-level appointees leave; it has less of an impact on the agency."
— *Frank Keating, former Governor, State of Oklahoma,*
and former General Counsel, Department of Housing
and Urban Development

"I measure success by the degree of change in an agency: the programs changed, if there are no scathing Inspectors General or GAO reports, if the appointee hasn't done anything to embarrass the administration. Avoid the appearance of scandal, real or trumped-up."
— *Charlie Grizzle, former Assistant Administrator*
for Administration and Resources Management,
Environmental Protection Agency

"As an appointee you should help build up your agency and leave it better than when you found it, as opposed to those appointees with no experience in government who want to use it to pursue their own agenda and in a fairly ruthless way. They use people and don't understand how bureaucracy functions. It takes so long to learn that they are gone before they do learn. We can't have two-year training programs in the government, senior officials who show up at the wrong meeting because they want to control everything—they gut their whole hierarchy by taking over and showing up inappropriately at lower-level meetings and taking over. They don't understand the system."
— *George H. W. Bush appointee*

3. Remember the White House

Relations with the White House, the Office of Management and Budget (OMB), and the Office of Personnel Management (OPM) require tremendous effort from PASs. Appointees feel a pull outward to the White House and a need to be responsive to the president who appointed them. Further, their rewards come from being a good team player. On the other hand, they feel a strong pull inward to be responsible leaders of their agency. In a time of constricting resources, it is often difficult to reconcile the two demands

---

On the White House

"It is important to have good relations with the White House. You want them to understand your mission, the good things you're producing for the president and the country. You want to open the doors and windows, explain your story, your goals, the change you want to bring—you have to do this all the time. The moment you get sick of explaining it is the moment the person you're explaining it to is begin-ning to get it—you have to keep doing it. The best policy has to be … explained over and over again."

— *Everett Ehrlich, former Under Secretary for*
Economic Affairs, Department of Commerce

"I figured the best way to help the president was to do a good job. The problem is that I have not been seen as part of the network or a team player…. I didn't accept White House personnel suggestions. I understand now that appointees have to be more politically sensitive than I was…."

— *George H. W. Bush appointee*

---

when, for example, the White House is demanding cutbacks at the expense of agency needs.

Elliot Richardson noted, "This government requires an element of trust and a high degree of comity to work. Washington is a city of cocker span-iels more ready to be loved and petted than to wield power." He continued, "Decision-making is the easiest thing I do, say one-seventh of the job. But once you make a decision you have to get the support of the staff, OPM, OMB, the Hill, interest groups, the president and the general public. All the players have to be at least considered and in some cases brought on board—the complexity of the governing process increases and grows faster than any of the trends that contribute to it.

"The function of the political process is to make choices among compet-ing claims. There are no simple answers or easy decision making and there is no objective way to decide among them. Any politician who doesn't waffle doesn't understand the problem. Politicians should have the imagination and intelligence and empathy to understand the jostling of competing claims." Ginger Ehn Lew, former deputy administrator of the Small Business

On OMB

"OMB has constrained our ability to be flexible. They are the embodiment of the control and accountability values in the bureaucracy. There are people there, both career and political, who are friendly to reinventing government concepts, but overall OMB has a gatekeeper mentality.... OMB will lay out flexible, innovative concepts, recruit candidates (agencies), get them on board, fine-tune it, and then remove the flexibility and keep the restrictions.... The budget people are the blockers, the career people generally. They have a gatekeeper mentality; they love to play the gotcha game. OPM for the most part is a huge obstacle, but there is a little cadre of supportive people there."

— *Bill Clinton appointee*

"In relation to OMB, mostly what I do is deal with conflict. OMB is very rigid and difficult to deal with, but that's their role and function and they do a good job at it. The department and OMB pre-screen my testimony before Congress and change it if they don't like it. Dancing to the tune of the political arena is all part of the bureaucracy."

— *George H. W. Bush appointee*

Administration, noted that in regard to the White House, "It's more a matter of personal relations than anything else, the same for Department of Commerce connections. It helps to have those connections because there's so much personal interaction in Washington."

"The appointee's job is to carry out the policies of the administration, respect the roles of the civil servants, and communicate with them," said Constance Berry Newman, current Assistant Secretary, Bureau of African Affairs, Department of State, and former director of the Office of Personnel Management. "Appointees serve only at the pleasure of the president. They can be fired instantly, there's no severance pay, there are two-year restrictions on employment in agencies you dealt with, some lobbying activities are barred for life. Given all this, the job kind of loses its charm."

And what happens when an appointee doesn't make the grade or commits political suicide? Ted Barreaux, former Counselor to the Comptroller General, General Accounting Office, noted, "Sometimes a person is just pushed out, he or she dies the death of a thousand cuts, sometimes self-inflicted." He noted one appointee in the George H. W. Bush administration who had ignored White House personnel suggestions, refused to have a White House liaison until they forced someone on her and then ignored her.

The Satisfaction of Public Service

Survey results indicate appointees' enjoyment of and satisfaction with their tenure in government and public service. They enjoyed dealing with challenging and interesting issues (98 percent reporting feeling generally and very greatly satisfied), making a difference and having an impact (95 percent), and meeting and working with stimulating people (94 percent). They liked working with both the career SES (88 percent) and their political colleagues (83 percent).

They also enjoyed managing in government (87 percent), especially the opportunity to improve agency operations (86 percent). They appreciated opportunities to promote the president's policy objectives (81 percent). They were generally happy with the quality of life in their agencies (68 percent), with the time requirements of their job (62 percent), and the amount of "down" time available to think creatively about the issues with which they deal (57 percent). They were satisfied with their relations with the White House (63 percent) and the news media (61 percent).

She turned to her friends in Congress to do an end run around the White House without telling them she'd already been turned down by the White House and so alienated her Hill support. Eventually, she had no friends left. His ominous warning, "If you alienate the White House, they'll get you. It may take three years, but they'll get you."

The power of OMB should be respected by political appointees. Said one Bill Clinton appointee, "As a manager, I consider OMB a necessary evil. OMB's powers of review are formidable." John Bartlett, former director of the Office of Civilian Radioactive Waste Management at the Department of Energy, notes, "There are 24 steps in the appropriations process, and OMB controls every gate in terms of what the administration brings to the Congress in that interaction."

Frank Keating, former Governor of Oklahoma and former general counsel, Department of Housing and Urban Development, noted, "White House intervention in agency affairs depends on the degree of interest of the president in the agency's issues.... HUD's relationship with OMB is difficult but professional. OMB sees itself as the self-proclaimed conscience and soul of the administration. In disputes between HUD and OMB, the White House counsel or others in the White House breaks the tie."

4. Collaborate with Congress

A federal bureaucracy that is lodged in the executive branch but overseen in the legislative is inherently cumbersome. Turf and political battles go with the bureaucratic territory, but if government is divided, as it has been for much of the past several decades, the partisan warfare can leave both career and political federal employees feeling like the proverbial grass trampled between two fighting elephants (or donkeys, as the case may be). As the African saying goes: "When elephants fight, it is the grass that suffers."

Our numbers reveal that in terms of dealing with the Congress, only 34 percent of the appointees considered it generally or very easy, while 37 percent considered it generally or very difficult. Additional research shows that only 57 percent declared themselves satisfied with their dealings with Congress, while 24 percent were generally or very dissatisfied.

A George H. W. Bush appointee noted, "There is a lack of clear direction of congressional oversight from the committees. The oversight hearings are muddled. You never know what to expect from them, but usually someone's going to get bloodied for political splash."

Oddly paired with lack of direction, he noted, "There is always micromanagement from the legislative branch. GAO is under the gun to produce this also. The fault-finding and micromanagement wear you down. Taking a chance and the risk of producing a mistake are not tolerated. You take constant berating and battering, and there's not much you can do about it—you don't have the leverage to make reform in the federal government. There's a lot of second guessing." The zero-defects-and-intolerance-for-error atmosphere of Washington combines infelicitously with the natural executive/legislative tension, but in this appointee's opinion, it was more an issue of turf than party.

On the other hand, Frank Hodsoll, former deputy director for management at the Office of Management and Budget and former chairman of the National Endowment for the Arts, observed, "You need at least some cooperation with Congress to get anything done." However, Michael J. Astrue, former general counsel of the Department of Health and Human Services, voiced the common feeling that "Congress has way overdone document requests. It simply demands too much documentation from the agencies, unnecessarily taking up far too much of our time and resources."

Inspectors general (IGs) walk a fine line between their assignment to weed out waste, fraud, and abuse, and the desire of many to use their critique to be helpful to their agencies, and the Congress, always looking for an excuse to beat up on an agency. Said one IG, "I haven't had the 'junk yard dog gotcha mentality' in my office. I set up a separate office of inspection and evaluation to tell the assistant secretaries how to correct problems they find. Program managers can ask for help from the unit, the unit gathers data, identifies problems and helps them evaluate how to fix problems. The problem is that the Congress has a 'gotcha' mentality and uses any report I issue that is critical of an agency to attack the agency and try to cut its budget."

Martin Kamarck, former Chair, Export-Import Bank of the United States, said, "Most senators know little about the issues and just want to beat up on an agency head because that's one of the perks of being a senator.... I didn't know the power of a member's staff to block my even getting an appointment with their boss if they wanted to and I didn't have the prior relationship to call the member directly and get through."

Not all appointees feel overwhelmed by the demands and hostility of the Congress. During his time in the executive branch, Anthony McCann, former Assistant Secretary for Management and Budget, Department of Veterans Affairs, recounted, "My relations with Congress were virtually nonexistent. The Hill doesn't understand much of what I do, so they left me alone. The VA has a culture of congressional staff dealing directly with the agency career budget director, so I rarely testified. The positive side of being left alone is that it kept me out of the line of fire when we do stupid things, and we did some stupid things. On the other hand, it has a negative side in that I have no mass of my own. My mass is entirely the secretary's. I can't act alone on a policy issue."

For a more detailed discussion on working with Congress, see chapter four.

"...It is important to remember that members of Congress, even of your party, are only loosely part of the same team. And the reason is that they are part of a separate branch of government that takes its role as a separate branch of government very seriously." (From Trattner, p. 27)
                                                                    — *Anonymous*

"Article I of the Constitution is the Congress. It is not the executive branch, it is not the judicial branch, it is the Congress. The founding fathers felt that was the seminal force for democracy—where the people had the direct authority to influence their lives in a pluralistic system.... everything emanates from that source of power." (From Trattner, p. 264)
                                                                    — *Anonymous*

"Congress is on a constant fishing expedition, demanding reams and reams of irrelevant information, demanding to have it yesterday at the latest, lots of oversight hearings. Congress is a pain in the neck, it's always overdoing oversight. They demand too much information and then they still hand out misinformation."

— Bill Clinton appointee

"All legislative powers are vested in Congress. Not most, not some, not domestic, but all legislative power is vested in Congress, and members of Congress take that seriously. Congress is much more ideological than the public generally is, and much more ideological than most members of the executive branch. Members of Congress are political.... The role of Congress is to be the forum in which differing points of view are debated, thought out, and one or the other prevails." (From Trattner, p. 11)

— Former member of the House

"Congress likes to hold hearings to yell about things. Congressmen are petty tyrants running a circus—hearings are shows to get headlines, publicity. They often display a willful ignorance of economics—hearings are grandstanding without knowing/learning the details. We waste money, time, and effort responding endlessly to congressional oversight rather than pursuing our mission."

— George H. W. Bush appointee

"I should have spent more time cultivating relationships with Congress. My attitude when I came in was 'I don't do Congress,' which was okay with my predecessor, who did it. However, when it hit the fan and my agency was under attack in Congress, I didn't have any backup. I hadn't built up trust ahead of time."

— Martin Kamarck

"Personally, I have great relations with the staff on the Hill. The key to being able to work in these jobs is respect for people and the job and roles that they have."

— Martha Krebs

"I know how the place works, I stick close to the committee and staff and keep them well informed. It makes them feel like proud parents, gives them ownership. Because I have made them crucial partners, I have good relationships with key staffers who are overlooked by White House staffers without Hill experience. They view Hill staffers as second-class citizens and only want to deal with the principal. But political appointees should realize that the staffers are the extension of power and authority of the member, they pass credit on to the Hill."
— *Bill Clinton appointee with previous Hill experience*

"Initiate contact with them. Say, 'I'm working on these topics and I know they are of concern to you, your district, your committee, you personally.... Ultimately, they need information from you about the topics that you deal with, so why not make it an open-ended offer to begin with?" (From Trattner, p. 32)
— *Former member of Congress*

5. Think Media

In a town in which the media is ever present, it can be surprising for appointees to learn the amount of effort required to get their story out to the public. The media can be your best ally in promoting your issue, but they can also be your worst enemy when something goes amiss. By consistently helping the media best do their job—by being available, by being forthright—you will benefit the most in both good times and bad. Still, it's always an uneasy alliance.

Appointees expressed a certain ambivalence about the media. Some 42 percent found dealing with it generally or very difficult, though 61 percent said they found their contact with the media satisfying. But as one George H. W. Bush IG said, "I have no or low respect for the media. I don't trust them. They are very interested in my reports but only as headline-grabbers ('Scandal at Agency X!')." Ivan Selin, former chair of the Nuclear Regulatory Commission, was something of an exception. He noted, "The media are the avenues to the people. Every public servant should consider it part of the job to deal with the media. It's the prime way to deal with their employers (the public). I have more sympathy for the media and Congress than do most appointees."

"The news cycle today is constant.... So there is terrible tension between getting the story right and getting it right away. You need to do both, but it's more important to get it right.... You've got to have your credibility. It's the most important thing, it's why you were brought into this government...." (From Trattner, p. 43)

— *Anonymous*

"You've got to understand that almost nobody in Washington is paying attention to your issue, regardless of how essential it is. You've got to break through the background clutter. You have to educate the media about your agency and its objectives. As a starter, better you invest an hour educating a reporter than try to get a story out." (From Trattner, p. 11)

— *Former agency head*

"Bad news is not like wine or cheese—it does not improve with age. You have a choice. Do you want to have a one-day story that says you screwed up? Or a three- or four-day story that says you screwed up and lied about how you screwed up and you tried to make it go away and it didn't go away? Better to just get it over with." (From Trattner, p. 39)

— *Anonymous*

"If there's a difference between government and private industry, it is in the ability to tell one's story. In government there is a sense that if you put out a press release once, it's enough. There isn't necessarily a sense of reinforcing it, of going back. There are great stories to be told." (From Trattner, p. 50)

— *Anonymous*

Susan M. Phillips, former governor of the Federal Reserve System, found a way to deal with the frustrations of dealing with "the fishbowl atmosphere in which you have to be careful about what you say, versus the university environment where freedom of speech is assumed, especially since the economy and market forces are so sensitive." After a bad experience with the media, Phillips says, "My frustration about being misinterpreted by a reporter and the subsequent effect on the stock market led me to cut way back on access to the press. But that isn't necessarily a healthy thing; you need to maintain a healthy balance. I use a text now when I give speeches and I give it to reporters so they can get it right. My talks are on futures or derivatives and are highly technical, so the press doesn't know as much about the subject and so rely on my text. They actually appreciate the help. It is more work but it's a good protection, and as a result, I have had fewer press problems than my peers who haven't learned that technique."

For a more detailed discussion on working with the media, see chapter five.

6. Pace Yourself

Washington is, in many ways, a tough town. It is difficult, particularly for people who come from outside the area, to find comfortable pockets of friendship, safe harbors to let off steam, or places simply to talk about something other than politics. There certainly is an awareness of the importance of dealing appropriately with stress. As William O. Studeman, former deputy director of the Central Intelligence Agency, noted, "Managing your health is a big issue around town. You have to avoid getting emotionally tied to it and develop stress management techniques, or this town will run you over and kill you deader than a doornail."

"I always feel stressed" is, unfortunately, a common feeling among appointees. As Admiral William Crowe, former Ambassador to the United Kingdom, observed, "Only in America are you presumed innocent until you're appointed by the president to a political position." As a new appointee, you will need to find ways to manage the stress you encounter.

"People in Washington tend to go to extremes about exercise," commented Martin Kamarck. "Either they are fanatics or they do nothing. There's lots to do in Washington but no real social life. Everything is politics; you have to watch yourself at all times, lest you let something slip out in an unguarded moment or behavior."

Another Bill Clinton appointee concurred: "You miss important family events, particularly when you're on the road. There are tensions between you and your spouse over your absences. It's really hard when I feel I am trying to do a good job, which entails travel, but I get the resentment at home, which, I must admit, I resent."

"The stress level is high," Studeman acknowledged. "You're used to doing it if you're already in town, but outsiders coming into town to take a political position might have a harder time adjusting to stress. You have to pick and choose priorities. There's also the social demands. My wife is an unpaid worker for the government."

With 60, 70, or even 80-hour weeks not uncommon, political government work is emotionally, physically, and intellectually draining. One Bill Clinton appointee attributed her high stress level to "the avalanche of things that have to be done: paper, meetings, different balls in the air, taking work home every night and weekend. The hours are intense—you don't know when the pressure's building up and the next thing you know, you've got a humongous cold or the flu. It's hard to feel like you can get away from it and totally relax. I work approximately 80 hours a week. I expected more of a slowdown after the letdown of the election win, but there has actually been more activity."

One George H. W. Bush appointee said that his stress level has been very high from day one. "The goal of most appointees by the end of the job is to leave one's job and get out of town with as few scars as possible. My job was listed as one of the 100 toughest jobs in government. With no annual leave or sick leave, you can't be out of touch, and if you are, you're in trouble. The IG watches you like a hound and has to investigate even anonymous allegations, no matter how far-fetched."

Roland Vautour agreed that there is a "very high level of stress among PASs. It comes from interest group pressure, Congress, self-imposed stress, stress coming from attempts to change things, when the status quo is the overriding influence in this town."

Philip Lee, former Assistant Secretary for Health in the Department of Health and Human Services, agreed with Vautour's assessment. "The hardest things to deal with are the growth and influence of the interest groups. I had been in health care policy for 30 years, but until now I didn't appreciate the magnitude of the interest group politics. I would have spent more time working with them before going forward with policy, I would have spent time hearing from them early on. The other major feature is the partisan polarization and political ideological hardening of positions, rather than problem solving."

One Bill Clinton appointee concurred with the conventional wisdom about the increasing political nastiness of Washington: "In 1994 when I came back, I found a more partisan, bitter, and petty town than when I left in 1981."

Everett Ehrlich also commented on the need to work the politics outside his agency: "I spent too much time doing internal management. I didn't realize how much you could use the constituency to mobilize support. The constituency of data users should be mobilized to support the programs they depend on. I needed earlier to develop a greater taste for going to lunch, put in the time and effort to nurture a network around town."

Rare though they are, there are those appointees who claim to have their stress under control. William Albrecht, former commissioner of the Commodity Futures Trading Commission, says he doesn't let stress get to him and is able to keep a sense of humor about it. "This is the least stress I've operated under. Deaning at a university was more stressful. I have no administrative duties here."

An overview of specific aspects of political appointees' jobs, shown in Table 2.5, on page 32, reveals varying levels of stress and frustration, including aspects highlighted in this chapter.

Table 2.5: How Easy or Difficult Do You Find Your Job?

Aspects of the Job	Generally and Very Easy	Neither Easy nor Difficult	Generally and Very Difficult
Managing a government organization or agency	30%	23%	47%
The substantive details of the policies with which I deal	38%	22%	40%
Decision making procedures of agency or department	31%	28%	41%
Directing senior career employees	63%	24%	13%
Defending my budget	39%	25%	37%
Defending my programs	48%	24%	28%
Dealing with the White House	47%	34%	19%
Dealing with OMB	35%	37%	28%
Dealing with Congress	34%	30%	37%
Dealing with the news media	42%	38%	20%

"Stress is a problem of the professional generation, but there are more workaholics in Washington than in any other place. They don't take time for families, so family problems arise. Health problems arise from not eating well and not exercising. It's the fast-track mentality—everyone's pretty much in a hurry. We'd do better jobs if we went a bit slower."
— *Paul Igaski, former Vice Chairman,*
Equal Opportunity Employment Commission

"I work 50 to 55 hours a week, but I don't have a hectic day. I have time to think about what I want to do. I delegate a great deal to the deputy assistant secretaries, unlike those who get swamped in minutiae and do not let it go. They deal with too much themselves."
— *Anthony McCann*

"I exercise and try to eat more reasonably; it's hard to do with all the dinners out. My divorce was largely caused by and added to the stress. We had to have a long-distance relationship and the marriage fell apart. It's impossible to have much time together; you don't solve problems if you don't have time together. You don't have a life, you don't have people in for dinner in Washington—you go out to restaurants."

— *Bill Clinton appointee*

"Your energy is the first thing government strips. It doesn't actually use your intellect—there's too much to do, too much to read, too much preparation required to make good use of one's intellect. Often I read material on the way to a meeting at which I have to make major financial decisions ... too much is decided on too little information. There is a lack of quality time to spend really thinking about the job."

— *George H. W. Bush appointee*

"The stresses ... are ... fatiguing. There are many more influences/ramifications due to interconnections with other government agencies. Now it's a mental and diplomatic exercise more than anything else. I cannot make a decision without doing it in a committee—it's not just based on objective factors, the best available information."

— *George H. W. Bush appointee*

"You have to live this, there's no way to know it otherwise. I didn't anticipate the level of stress. I've had stress before, but this is Olympic stress. What's most frustrating is not having a clear shot at making a decision, no authority to make a final decision—hundreds of people have the power to block any decision."

— *George H. W. Bush appointee*

7. Enjoy the Job

Despite the frustrations inherent in government service, appointees find many satisfactions in it. Ginger Lew values, "Being able to implement policies that make a real difference in peoples' lives, such as our microlending programs. For example, there was a woman who was in a shelter, a victim of domestic violence. We gave her a loan so she could start a small business selling lapel pins. She now has $1 million in annual sales and employs 20 women who were all victims of domestic violence. This is good stuff, there are great success stories to share."

The chance to work in a particular area of expertise with colleagues one respects attracts many. Reflecting on her time at the Department of Interior,

"One's personal life is so compromised, there's not enough time to see friends—it's crazy, totally insane. Protect some of that time more, don't respond to every request. Delegate or turn down requests—it's hard for a new person to do, but it's absolutely essential."

— *Philip Lee*

"Washington is a very demanding, expensive town. The in-crowd social expectations could easily dominate your entire life."

— *George H. W. Bush appointee*

"I get a real sense of satisfaction from suggesting change and having it implemented. It's like golf—you get one or two good shots a round and you keep coming back."

— *Charles Baquet*

"You're far more involved in critical issues than if you work in the private sector."

— *Anthony McCann*

"I feel the loss of ambition and money are offset by the challenge the work provides, the ability to have a positive impact, the opportunity to make a difference. There is no similar opportunity outside of government."

— *Pamela Talkin, former member,*
Federal Labor Relations Authority

"Being a PAS opened a world to me that I didn't know existed—it was an adventure and important on substantive grounds, as well."

— *Sharon Robinson, former Assistant Secretary,*
Office of Education Research and Improvement,
Department of Education

Bonnie Cohen said, "It was an opportunity to make a difference in an area (the environment) that I think is a critical area." Doyle Cook, former board member, Farm Credit Administration, noted the satisfaction of "being able to put into practice what I've learned over the years, developing policies, fixing situations." For Nicolas P. Retsinas, former assistant secretary for housing at the Department of Housing and Urban Development, the satisfaction came from "the opportunity to be at the table for every housing issue facing the country."

Anthony McCann found his "greatest sources of satisfaction are relations with the staff and redemption of lost souls (careerists who have been sidelined or shunted aside). Once placed in different positions where their skills match the job, where they are given something meaningful to do where their skills are best used, they have flourished."

One George H. W. Bush appointee enjoyed being an agent for change in his job. He was able to use his negotiation skills from his prior work at the Federal Bureau of Investigation and found satisfaction in reaching compromise to problem solve. He even enjoyed political work and working with Congress. Another spoke of the challenge of the job itself as reason enough, despite a large loss he sustained in retired military pay.

A George H. W. Bush appointee noted: "It's an honor to serve the president, an opportunity to operate at a senior executive level I mightn't have had otherwise. It's not a second career, it's a presidential appointment for a finite duration." Said William Albrecht, "It's a great experience. However, the opportunity to feel you've done something is less than it is in academia where one can build up a program or develop a school. You have to create those opportunities to do something." Frank Hodsoll said he simply enjoyed "getting things done. It's a lot less money but a lot more fun than if I'd stayed in the law firm." Another George H. W. Bush appointee said, "It's the most exciting job I've ever had in my life—there's never been a boring moment."

"Has it been a good experience? I don't know. Am I glad I did it? Yes," said Ada Deer, former Assistant Secretary for Indian Affairs at the Department of Interior. Remarked Edward Gleiman, former chairman of the Postal Rate Commission, "Would I do it again? You bet, it's been frustrating but fun."

CHAPTER THREE

Getting to Know You: Rules of Engagement for Political Appointees and Career Executives

Joseph A. Ferrara
Director, Master of Policy Management Program
Georgetown Public Policy Institute
Georgetown University

Lynn C. Ross
Doctoral Candidate in American Government
Georgetown University

This report was originally published in January 2005.

Introduction

Every four years in the United States, a new presidential administration enters office or an existing administration starts its second term. Either way, new political executives assume a variety of positions throughout the federal government. Indeed, new political appointees[1] are constantly coming in and out of government service, not just immediately after elections. This approach to government management is somewhat unique to the American system—few other nations put so much power in the hands of a relatively small number of people, none of whom is a career government employee.

According to the Government Accountability Office (GAO), the average tenure in office of presidential appointees is just under three years (other reports calculate a somewhat lower number).[2] In his 1987 study of political appointees, G. Calvin Mackenzie referred to them as the "in-and-outers:"

> From the earliest days of the United States as a nation, the highest-ranking administrators of the federal government have been drawn largely from a category of people known in federal parlance as "in-and-outers," individuals for whom government service is neither a profession nor a career (p. xiii).

The "in-and-outer" system serves some very important political purposes, such as giving the president an opportunity to reward loyal political supporters with plum assignments and to bolster his position within his own party by appointing people who represent key ideological constituencies. But the key significance of the appointee system is that it gives the president the crucial ability to shape his leadership team as he assumes power over the federal government.

Since the passage of the 20th Amendment to the Constitution, which moved Inauguration Day from March to January, presidential transitions in the American system have been notoriously brief (and the contested election of 2000, of course, put even more pressure on an already tight schedule). Election Day occurs on the first Tuesday in November; about 11 weeks later, the president is inaugurated as chief executive. The president must quickly assemble a governing team. Explicit in the president's considerations is the notion that his appointees are people he can trust to faithfully articulate and implement his political agenda. But there are implicit considerations, too. These include the belief that the president's appointees will be responsible stewards of the public trust and competent managers of the federal departments and agencies they are asked to lead.

But of course the president does not just rely on the political executives to run the government—the administrative state is just too big and complex. Once the appointees take office, they assume control of agencies staffed by career government employees.[3] These careerists[4] perform an incredibly diverse array of tasks; civil servants are economists, lawyers, doctors, air traffic controllers, scientists, policy analysts, budget examiners, regulators, administrative assistants, sociologists, construction workers—the list goes on and on. Overall, there are about 1.8 million career civilian employees throughout the federal government (not counting the U.S. Postal Service). Over 120,000 of them are senior managers.[5] At the very top of the career pyramid are about 6,000 members of the career Senior Executive Service (SES).[6] These two groups of senior career civil servants interact most frequently with political appointees, and therefore make up the population we focus on. (Tables 3.1 and 3.2 show the number and type of senior career officials and political appointees.)

Both senior careerists and political appointees are highly educated. More than 90 percent of each group has at least a college degree—more than half of political appointees have an advanced or professional degree, and two-thirds of senior career executives have this level of education. Careerists tend to be about eight years older than political appointees, and unlike their political counterparts, most of their career has been in the federal government. (Table 3.3 on page 40 and 3.4 on page 41 provide demographic profiles of the two groups.)[7]

In many ways, careerists represent the institutional memory of American public administration. They are public administration's cartographers,

Table 3.1: Type and Numbers of Senior Career Employees*

Rank	Number
GS-14	76,866
GS-15	39,579
SES	5,962
Total	122,407

Source: U.S. Office of Personnel Management Fact Book (http://www.opm.gov/feddata/03factbk.pdf; accessed 10/25/04) and www.opm.gov/feddata/02paystru.pdf; accessed 10/25/04)

*We include GS-14s and GS-15s in this table for the sake of completeness. While most of our career interviewees were members of the SES (either current or former), it is true that senior GS employees also interact with political executives, albeit not as frequently. Also, the nature and structure of the interaction can be somewhat different. For example, while career SES members may in fact report directly to a political appointee, most senior GS-14s and GS-15s will not.

Table 3.2: Type and Numbers of Political Appointees

Type	Number
PAS	1,203
PA	223
NA	648
LA	169
SC	1,287
Total	3,530

PAS: Presidential appointments requiring Senate confirmation
PA: Presidential appointments without Senate confirmation
NA: Senior Executive positions filled by non-career appointment
LA: Limited term SES appointments (some of which can be career)
SC: Schedule C Excepted Appointments

Source: The 2000 Plum Book (www.gpoaccess.gov/plumbook/2000/index.html; accessed 10/26/04)

Table 3.3: Profile of the Career Senior Executive Service (2002)

Average age	53.8
Average length of service (years)	25.5
Education Not college graduate College graduate Advanced degree	5% 29% 66%
Gender Men Women	75% 25%
Minority	14%
Occupation Scientist or engineer Other professional Administrative/technical	21% 22% 57%
Geographic location Washington, D.C. area	76%

Note: *Percentages may not add to 100 because of rounding.*

Source: *U.S. Office of Personnel Management Fact Book (http://www.opm.gov/feddata/03factbk. pdf; accessed 10/25/04)*

drawing the maps for new administrations that connect the administrative present with the past. For political appointees interested in the future, such policy maps can be an invaluable resource.

So the president must rely on two groups of people to run the government: political appointees and career civil servants. It is not an exaggeration to say that, perhaps more than anything else, effective governance in the American political system depends critically on whether and how these two groups develop a healthy and productive working relationship. They must get to know each other, learn to trust each other, and figure out how to communicate clearly with one another. This can be difficult because political appointees and career civil servants, while they both share an overriding commitment to public service, are very different in many other respects.

An important challenge is reconciling different conceptions of public service. There is no question that most political appointees and careerists are intensely committed to the public service. But their conceptions of public service differ in important ways. The vast majority of careerists have no political aspirations (indeed, many of the career executives we interviewed went out of their way to avoid "politics"). This does not mean that they are not ambitious; in fact, many careerists work hard for promotions and want

Table 3.4: Profile of Political Appointees*

Average age	45.9
Government service (years)	9.14
Education Not college graduate College graduate Advanced degree	 6% 41% 52%
Gender Men Women	 73% 27%
Minority	18%

Note: Percentages may not add to 100 because of rounding.

Source: In the Web of Politics: Three Decades of the Federal Executive, *Aberbach and Rockman, 2000, pp. 58-79.*

* *These data were gathered in 1992, and thus do not directly reflect the current cadre of political appointees. It is assumed, however, that they are representative of, or at least similar to, the current demographics for political appointees. While OPM keeps current statistics on the federal career workforce, it unfortunately does not do the same for political executives. And, beyond Aberbach and Rockman, there are not many other extant profiles of political appointees. In 1999, the IBM Center for The Business of Government published a survey of federal executives that included 47 non-career respondents. These results track pretty closely with the Aberbach-Rockman data. For example, in the IBM survey, non-career respondents were, on average, 48 years old, mostly men (64%), and had spent about nine years in government.*

to have some influence in the public policy process, particularly within internal agency debates. It simply means that their conception of public service does not include, or at least emphasize, political and ideological advocacy. Rather, a civil servant's notion of public service is typically more centered on issues like ensuring that policy makers benefit from technically competent advice and managing fair and open processes of government. As one of our career interviewees said, "Our job is to help make sure that political appointees don't make uninformed decisions."

Political appointees have a different conception of public service. Unlike their careerist counterparts, they are much more openly political. They declare allegiance to one of the two major parties.[8] They align themselves with the political and programmatic agenda of a particular president. They advocate for particular policy outcomes. While it might be said that careerists are more focused on the means of government, political appointees are more focused on its ends. Careerists are there to do the nation's business; political appointees are there to determine what the nation's business should be. To the extent that these differing conceptions of public service can be reconciled to establish a productive working relationship, the more likely it is that an administration will be successful in implementing its agenda.

Part of reconciling these different conceptions of public service is acknowledging that they exist in the first place, which is another way of saying that political appointees and careerists need to understand their respective roles in the policy process. But this is not enough. Political appointees and career employees must also overcome the myths that they each tend to have about the other. What gives myths their power is that they tap into strong beliefs that people already hold about the way the world works—or ought to work.

But quite often myths are based on exceptions or what linguists call "synecdoche." A synecdoche is a figure of speech in which a part is substituted for the whole, and its use in political rhetoric is legion.[9] Thus, the $400 hammer comes to represent wasteful military spending and the "welfare queen" comes to represent wasteful domestic spending. Similarly, a political appointee's encounter with a sleepy or inattentive career employee at a staff meeting might reinforce a pre-existing belief that careerists are low-energy workers more interested in job security than high performance, and a careerist's encounter with an incompetent political appointee whose main qualification for office seems to be his or her prolific campaign contributing might confirm an assumption that appointees are just political hacks uninterested in the details of policy and governance. But just as the $400 hammer and the "welfare queen" do not represent what actually happens in most defense and social programs, the stereotypical lazy government worker and the ambitious but unqualified political appointee are more myth than reality. That such myths exist is undeniable; the challenge is overcoming them so that effective working relationships can be formed.

Political appointees and career civil servants are different in other ways, too (some of the key differences are summarized in Table 3.5). Political appointees come in and go out of government service far more often than career civil servants. Political appointees serve, on average, about two to three years in any one office and average about nine total years of government service. The average length of government service for senior career executives, by contrast, is over 25 years.[10]

Given the significant variation in tenure in office, it is not surprising that political appointees and career civil servants also have different time perspectives. Political executives tend to be much more focused on the short term; they cannot assume that the president they serve will be in office for more than one administration; and even if he is, they cannot assume they themselves will be in office that long. Career executives, on the other hand, tend to have a longer time perspective; they have worked in their respective agencies far longer than the political managers they work for.

Another area of difference is professional experience. Political appointees, by definition, come in and out of government. Many of them have worked in government before, but they have also worked outside the public sector,

Table 3.5: Political Appointees and Career Civil Servants

Factor	Political appointees	Careerists
Role perception	• "Determine the nation's business" • Focused on achieving policy outcomes	• "Do the nation's business" • Focused on ensuring a fair, open, and sound decision process
Partisanship	• Affiliated with a political party • Serve a particular president	• Nonpartisan on the job • Serve various presidents
Professional experience	• Often a mix of government, academic, and private sector	• Government has been their main carer
Tenure of service	• Come in and go out • Average about two years in their positions, about four years in their agency, and about nine years of government service	• In for the long term • Senior executives average four years in their positions, 19 years in their agency, and more than 25 years of government service
Time perspective	• Tend to have a shorter-term outlook	• Tend to have a longer-term outlook

including in academia, nonprofit think tanks, and for-profit firms.[11] Career managers, by contrast, tend to build their professional careers in the public sector.

Research Process and Structure of the Chapter

Over the last half of 2004, we interviewed numerous political appointees and careerists, including people still serving in government, as well as former officials. We talked to them in one-on-one interview meetings[12] where we could explore one person's perspective in depth, and we have held focus group sessions where groups of political appointees or civil servants were able to exchange ideas and share their personal experiences and reflections on public service. In addition to these interviews,[13] we reviewed relevant books, articles, and reports that deal with the subject of political/ career interaction.

The structure of the chapter is as follows. First, we explore the myths that each group sometimes holds about the other (or, perhaps more accurately, that each group thinks the other holds about them). For example, at the beginning of a new administration, careerists often say they feel that the incoming political appointees automatically assume the careerists are loyal to the previous administration, regardless of whether any evidence to suggest such loyalty actually exists. We try to look behind the mythology to see what drives such perceptions and how widespread they really are.

Second, we develop some "rules of engagement" for political appointees and career civil servants. Our goal is to develop a common-sense approach that both groups can use to begin (and sustain) their relationship on a positive note that emphasizes their joint commitment to public service. Included in these sections are two case studies based on recent events that illustrate the consequences of failure to heed these rules. The first deals with former National Park Police Chief Teresa Chambers. The second case involves Medicare Actuary Richard Foster.

Finally, we offer some key findings and recommendations that summarize the myths and rules of engagement broadly and synthesize our research findings with other findings from the literature.

Myths about Career Civil Servants

In this section, we highlight some of the myths that are most detrimental to a political appointee's ability to hit the ground running. Perhaps here we can short-circuit some preconceived notions, thus allowing political appointees to get right to the business of governing. The myths and the corresponding realities are summarized in Table 3.6 on page 50 at the end of this section.

Myth 1: Careerists are loyal to the previous administration.

The career executives we interviewed expressed some frustration with having to prove their trustworthiness each time a presidential administration changes. Having been through many transitions, however, most career executives expect this "dance." This particular element of distrust stems from politics. Specifically, appointees sometimes assume careerists' personal political beliefs and loyalties influence the way they do their jobs.

Questioning the political loyalty of the career civil service is not a new phenomenon in American politics. Presidency scholar Richard Neustadt, who advised John F. Kennedy on his 1960 transition, warned that "incomers" tend to have the impression "that their inherited civil servants could be covert enemies, planted on them by their predecessors (whose party just lost the election)."[14]

But Neustadt argued that such suspicion is a bar to knowledge because it prevents appointees from using one of their most valuable governing resources—the "lore" or institutional memory of the civil service staff.

The evidence suggests that career executives focus more on the policies and the nuts and bolts of the work than on the politics. In many cases, careerists told us that the political affiliation of the appointees for whom they worked actually mattered a lot less than the appointee's personal style. As one focus group participant put it, "[the] challenge is simply that you have a new boss to get used to … it's not necessarily a career/political thing."

Careerists also have a strong sense of the role they are supposed to play in the federal system. "We [civil servants] understand the Constitution," said one of our interviewees. Many careerists spoke of the administration (whatever administration it is) as having the right to make its mark on the government by virtue of its electoral legitimacy. There is a sense among careerists that an important part of doing their job is serving the agenda of the current president *because* he is the current president and regardless of his party.

In general, we found that careerists check their personal politics at the door because they view their role in the political process as technical, not partisan. Another high-level careerist echoed these sentiments:

> [Career employees] know the job. If you're not in a position to do what your political masters want you to do, then you shouldn't be working in that kind of a high-level policy job to begin with. You know that administrations are going to change. You know that at least half the time you'll have a boss whose political philosophy is different from your own. If you can't cope with that, you ought to go and do something else. I think that's the way most people behave.

When a new administration is from a different political party than the previous one, the problem of mistrust is exacerbated. One interviewee said of the George W. Bush appointees, "When we [civil servants] talked, all they heard was Clinton-Gore." Careerists are dismayed by this mentality because they view their role as technical advisers to all administrations, helping to guide appointees through the policy process, not setting political agendas. Because of their role, careerists value their technical credibility. When political appointees assume careerists have a political bent or misplaced loyalty, it undermines careerists' sense of having credibility.

Again, this issue is not new to American politics. In fact, since presidential transitions were shortened more than 50 years ago, the political loyalty of the civil service has been questioned.[15] Richard Neustadt reported that:

> Mistrust of the civil servants in 1953 was understandable, considering that many of their agencies had come into existence in the generation since Republicans had held the White House. Actually Washington bureaucrats, like their fellow countrymen, voted for Ike in droves and keenly anticipated his arrival. But that was not instantly apparent to incomers who had been brought up hating Roosevelt….[16]

One interviewee captured the overall sentiment we heard from many we talked to about where careerists' loyalties lie: "Career employees try to carry out the policies of whatever administration is in office. If they feel strongly against a policy, they would be more likely to change jobs. If there's something that is against your moral fiber ... you don't sabotage [the policy or the appointee], because your first obligation is to the government of the United States." Another said that careerists would tend to speak up against policies they didn't like, but once a decision is made, "they would salute and do their best to implement and enforce the policies."

Myth 2: Careerists are not passionate about their work and they don't work that hard.

The careerists we interviewed expressed a strong degree of dedication— to their organizations, policy arenas, and to public service more generally. They also expressed their willingness to work hard, and pointed out a history of working long hours under often stressful conditions. According to some of the careerists, appointees often assume that civil servants will not go the extra mile to get the job done. This perception may stem from the difference in perceived time frames between careerists and political appointees.

One career interviewee told us about his experience working on a major policy review commissioned by the incoming George H.W. Bush administration in 1989. The review was led by political appointees but largely staffed

---

What Political Appointees Said about Careerists

First Impressions

"[At first,] they were skeptical of me and our agenda."

"Very risk averse."

"Seemed tentative and afraid to give their real opinions."

"Too much focus on process."

"I was at a research organization, and the staff was highly knowledgeable and motivated."

"I valued their input."

"They seemed very eager to please."

"Some of the careerists thought we were crazy!"

Later Impressions and Insights

"They wanted to play in the policy process."

"The civil servants really trained me."

"They really responded to good management."

"Most of them understood that I belonged at the table to fight for certain policies."

by senior career officials (SES and GS-15 levels). It was expected, although never verbalized explicitly, that the review staff would work whatever hours were required to make sure the process was comprehensive and to meet the deadline for submitting a final report to the White House. "We worked long hours, including weekends and federal holidays. No one complained. Everyone was excited about being part of a major policy review at the beginning of a new administration."

One career executive said, "They [political appointees] are running a sprint and we [career civil servants] are running a marathon." Another careerist characterized an important difference by calling civil servants "WEBEHWYGs" (which he pronounced "WEE-BEE-WIGS") or "We'll be here when you're gone." Although this characterization implies that civil servants would feel less than compelled to follow a political appointee's directives, this is not what the evidence shows. The vast majority of political appointees we talked to found careerists competent, responsive, and dedicated to the work.

Myth 3: Careerists work in government service because of the security their positions offer.

Many of our career interviewees said that public service was an important factor in keeping them on the job. When careerists are cut out of decision making or prevented from playing a role in the management of programs and the formulation of policy, their job satisfaction is diminished because they feel impeded from playing the public service role they value. Interestingly, several of the political appointees whom we interviewed found it very surprising that careerists did not behave as advocates of certain policies. One former appointee said, "I don't know how they [careerists] remain so neutral when decisions are made that run counter to their recommendations. I couldn't do it." This is a perfect characterization of the different role perceptions that each group holds.

Understanding what motivates careerists is as important as understanding what *doesn't* motivate them. "My [political boss] took me to the Hill for high-level meetings and this was a real motivator," said one focus group participant. Another career interviewee talked about his experience attending a bill-signing ceremony at the White House: "We all had worked very hard on this legislation, and it made me feel good to be invited to the ceremony." Similar sentiments were expressed in our interviews where careerists reported greater satisfaction when they worked on key initiatives that they knew were important and meaningful.

Having said this, there is no question that senior careerists understand the value of their civil service protections. While the Civil Service Reform

Act of 1978, which established the Senior Executive Service, gave political appointees more power to move SES members around from position to position (and even, in theory, from agency to agency), Title 5 of the U.S. Code still prohibits a new administration from dislocating a career SES member during the first 120 days of its term of office. Several of our SES interviewees mentioned this legal protection as an important part of ensuring a productive political/career working relationship. The 120-day "waiting period" in effect forces new political appointees and career executives to get to know each other, because it does not allow incoming appointees to simply begin arbitrarily or capriciously moving careerists around.

Thus, while job security is a consideration, as it probably is for most people, career executives are not preoccupied with it. One high-level careerist said that the motivations of most of her colleagues are a combination of "wanting to do their best work and having a strong interest in the field they're working in." Although she also mentioned that "stability is essential for living" and "you can't do the job for free," she argued that so-called extrinsic rewards (like money) are not the main reasons for staying on the job. Instead, it's the intellectual stimulation, dealing with other people, and solving problems that are the most important motivators for service. Another career interviewee, a senior official working at the notoriously drab Pentagon building, said, "If they took my window away at this point, I think I'd retire, but the extrinsic stuff is not the prime motivator [for doing this job]. I think stimulation and dealing with other people, solving problems, is the prime motivator."

Myth 4: Careerists want to obstruct change—they are naysayers.

Careerists tend to be well steeped in the details of the policy areas and programs on which they work. Career executives in particular have risen within the merit system of their organizations because of their technical expertise.[17] They are likely to have substantial organizational expertise (knowing who is who and how the component parts interact); understand the historical background of policies and programs; and possess a long and deep institutional memory.

These traits can be very beneficial to organizations in transformation because these employees have thought about and often personally experienced the hurdles associated with making change. One careerist said, "[Appointees] are well intentioned but often naive. They are not aware of the real limitations—[we] had to educate them as to their limitations." Another said that appointees sometimes come to office with "a lot of breathless ideas."

Unfortunately, appointees sometimes see this detail-oriented perspective as small-picture thinking and inertia. Careerists, for their part, see limitations and details as an important part of the policy formulation and implementation processes. This disconnect between roles and perceptions of careerists and appointees often creates the misperception among political appointees that careerists prefer the status quo or say no for its own sake, which can cause tension between the two groups.

One of our career interviewees offered a novel approach for building trust with political appointees. Rather than pester the political executives with all the reasons that a particular approach has not worked successfully in the past, this careerist suggested the following: "Political appointees are like teenagers. Sometimes you have to let them make their own mistakes."

Political appointees, at least initially, tend to see the bureaucracy as a barrier to getting their job done. From an appointee's perspective, it makes sense to translate "we've tried that before and it didn't work" into "I'm not going to help you implement your agenda." Unfortunately, the message that careerists send is often misread. The career executives we interviewed were sensitive to being perceived as naysayers when political appointees propose ideas for change. Many of our career interviewees argued that they try to give appointees a realistic sense of the limitations that exist given the organizational, political, technical, or policy-related problems. This cautious posture is often an effort to prevent political appointees from setting themselves up for failure. One career executive said, "You have to walk a fine line. You can't come out and say [to an appointee] that this [idea] just won't work."

Perhaps the lesson in this misunderstanding cuts both ways: Careerists need to be sensitive to how they deliver "the bad news" about the practical limitations of certain proposals, and political appointees need to assume that the careerists' warnings are delivered with the best of intentions. In short, careerists want their political bosses to succeed, and pointing out the potential pitfalls is one way they add value to that endeavor.

Myth 5: Careerists do not really want their political bosses to succeed.

Presidents have always recognized the importance of having successful political appointees who enjoy good reputations. Shortly after he became the nation's first president, George Washington said, "If injudicious or unpopular measures should be taken by the Executive under the New Government with regards to appointments, the Government itself would be in the utmost danger of being utterly subverted by the measures."

Careerists also want the political appointees for whom they work to succeed. There are several reasons for this. First, careerists tend to care about their organization's reputation. Nothing tarnishes an organization's reputation faster than an unsuccessful appointee (recall the severe image problems that controversial appointees like Ann Burford at the Environmental Protection Agency and James Watt at the Department of the Interior caused for their agencies during the Reagan administration). Perhaps careerists care about their organization's reputation because it reflects on them personally and professionally, but nonetheless, they seem to have a strong stake in it.

Second, careerists care about adding value to the process. If a careerist's political boss does not accomplish his or her goals, this diminishes the careerist's perception that he or she is contributing. In this sense, the failure of the political agenda becomes the failure of the career agenda.

Third, an unsuccessful appointee is probably an unhappy appointee, and an unhappy appointee is probably an unpleasant manager, which erodes the quality of work life. Ultimately careerists, like most people, want to please their bosses. This gives them a sense of accomplishment and fulfillment. If they are dismayed by the direction the political appointee is going, they likely will leave that particular organization and find some place where they fit in better.

Table 3.6: Myths (and Realities) about Career Civil Servants

Myth	Reality
Careerists are loyal to the previous administration.	• Most careerists check their politics at the door and define their role in terms of the policy process, not the administration's political agenda. • Most careerists see their role as technical, not partisan.
Careerists don't work hard.	• Most careerists work extremely hard under tight deadlines and often stressful conditions. • Careerists are "running a marathon"; political appointees are "running a sprint."
Careerists are mostly interested in job security.	• Most careerists are motivated by a strong sense of public service, mission dedication, participation in the policy process, and intellectual challenge.
Careerists always say no to new ideas.	• Most careerists are not "against" new policy ideas but are sensitive to the various implementation challenges. • Careerists' many years of experience have conditioned them to see change in very pragmatic terms.
Careerists want their political bosses to fail.	• Most careerists want their political executives to succeed because they believe in the system and because they want their agencies to succeed.

Myths about Political Appointees

Just as political appointees sometimes make unwarranted assumptions about the career managers they supervise, careerists sometimes assume certain things about political appointees that are usually more mythology than reality. This section explores the roots of these myths. The myths, and corresponding realities, are summarized in Table 3.7 on page 55 at the end of this section.

Myth 1: Political appointees care only about ideology and don't really worry about organizational stewardship.

We asked the careerists we interviewed to recall their first impressions of the political appointees they had worked with over the years. One persistent impression—often disproved over time—was that the incoming political appointees did not really care about the organization they were taking charge of, particularly in the sense of leaving the agency a better place than they found it. Rather, careerists often sense that the new political executive is worried mostly, if not exclusively, about achieving the ideological agenda of the administration. In this view, the agency itself and the careerists who populate it are just tools political appointees can use to achieve their objectives.

This is a powerful myth because it seems to fit with the objective reality. After all, political appointees do come in and out of government with great regularity and quite often they do not stay very long. Some appointees return to private life while others move on to other jobs within the administration. And, simply by virtue of their political connection with the party currently occupying the White House, there seems to be little doubt that appointees are more focused on achieving a set of policy objectives than on maintaining and enhancing the agency they lead.

One careerist told us that while he had worked with many conscientious political appointees over the years, he had more than once encountered an appointee "who seemed very political—always watching out for the interests of the groups he used to work with before he came into government." Another careerist who has worked in several transitions, including the most recent from Clinton to Bush, said that the "getting to know you" phase of transitions is normal, but that some of the transitions he had worked in were complicated by incoming political executives who "were too ideological and did not want any help from the career staff."

Of course, political executives must worry about the policy agenda of the White House. In a very real sense, that is exactly why they are in their jobs in the first place. But truly effective political appointees understand that they must earn the trust of the career managers they lead. One way of doing this is by taking on the role of organizational steward. Many of the political appointees we talked to seemed to understand this. Worrying about organizational maintenance, in their view, is more than just good management—it also sends a powerful message to the career staff that the political leadership understands their value, the value of the larger organization, and the value of government as a whole.

Myth 2: Political appointees are not really competent to do the jobs to which they're appointed.

Another powerful myth about appointees is that they are simply political hacks who have gotten their jobs because of their party connections or campaign work.[18] According to this myth, political appointees are not really qualified or competent to lead the agencies to which they are appointed. Rather, they enter office naive, ill-informed, and unrealistic about what can be accomplished in a brief four-year presidential term. This mythology explains the sense of tension and mutual wariness that often characterizes the initial period as political appointees and careerists get to know each other.

Again, the general conclusion of many of the careerists we interviewed was that highly competent political appointees were much more often the rule than the exception. But, of course, the exceptions are what help stoke the mythology. One careerist talked about an assistant secretary appointee who took over a very technical research and engineering staff but had no academic or practical training in the subject matter. There was a great deal of cynicism about this appointee among the staff, and the skepticism was heightened by the appointee's political connections. According to this careerist, "This guy was nice and easy to work with, but it was pretty clear that he was a politician and not a technocrat. He had been a big contributor to the presidential campaign and had served as an elected official himself earlier in his career."

Are there appointees who are not competent for the jobs they take? Surely there are, just as there are people in every line of work who sometimes are hired into jobs for which they are not really qualified. But the vast majority of presidential appointees are very competent for their positions.[19] In some cases, appointees come from academia, where they have been researching and teaching a particular policy area for years before assuming office. Sometimes appointees arrive from senior positions in the private sector, where they have overseen large government contracts or worked with the government on regulatory enforcement and managed large organizations. And, of course, many appointees have served in government before.[20]

Several of the political appointees we talked to not only had prior policy-specific experience but also had direct experience working with the agency they were now leading. In some cases, their prior experience was as a customer of the research services produced by the agency. In other cases, we interviewed political appointees who had previously served as career

What Careerists Said about Political Appointees

First Impressions

"[During the transition] the transition team seems to be still in campaign mode, not governing mode."

"In some cases, their résumés did not match the job they were taking."

"Initially, there seemed to be a lot of tension and suspicion, on both sides."

"They [the appointees] weren't sure who to trust at first."

"[Political appointees] didn't understand the real limitations of what they could accomplish."

"Some appointees don't understand the culture or the politics of the department they are entering."

Later Impressions and Insights

"The person really grew into the job."

"They were more moderate in their opinions than I first thought."

"I was struck by how some of our appointees came to see the career staff in a positive light."

"Feedback is tough because many appointees do not want to make policy in an open forum."

civil servants in the very same agency to which they were appointed. As people who had been on both sides of the relationship, these individuals have a particularly interesting perspective.

One political appointee who previously served as a careerist told us that his perspective completely changed when he took on the political job. For one thing, he was struck at what he called "the cynicism of the career staff"—"they seemed to assume that all policy and programmatic decisions were being made for political reasons; any deviation from their analytical recommendations was immediately taken as a political compromise." This interviewee admitted that he himself had harbored such thoughts during his days as a careerist, but once he assumed the role of political executive, he realized that he had a much wider view of issues than he did as a careerist. Yes, compromises did sometimes have to be made, but not just for "political" reasons. Many times, there was new information brought to bear on the decision that was not accessible to his career analysts. He went on to note that this example illustrates why it is so important for political appointees to provide good feedback to their career partners. In the absence of feedback and good information, it is natural for careerists to assume that "behind closed door" politics is at work, not rational decision making.

In addition to our interviews, several studies bear this out. For example, a prior examination of a National Academy for Public Administration presidential appointee database showed that, as a group, most political appointees tend to be very well educated and enter office with prior public service credentials.[21] (In fact, more and more appointees come from the Washington, D.C. metropolitan area, having previously served as congressional staff members or even career civil servants. This is significant because it is more evidence that, contrary to the mythology, political appointees are typically very well versed in the workings of government.)[22]

Myth 3: Political appointees do not want to hear information that contradicts their ideological agendas.

This myth is closely linked with the notion that political appointees care more about ideology than organizational stewardship. In this view, because political appointees are mostly focused on narrow policy agendas, they do not want to hear any information that might contradict their ideological position. Thus a Defense appointee who comes into office arguing that there are too few people in the military does not want to hear that the real problem might not be the overall number of recruits as much as it is the types of skills the recruits bring with them. In this hypothetical example, Defense careerists might decide that they should keep their data to themselves and not raise arguments against the political executive's stated position.

Many of the careerists we interviewed had encountered such ideologically driven appointees at one point or another. But, again, this was the exception and not the rule. Moreover, several of our political interviewees argued that they encouraged their careerists to, in the words of one appointee, "disprove my hypothesis." This appointee argued that the decisions he makes are far too important and consequential to be decided solely on the basis of political ideology. His approach is to state his working hypothesis for how to solve a particular policy problem and then ask the career staff to try to "disconfirm" this hypothesis with hard data. In his view, there are two important elements here. First, he is showing the careerists that he wants and values their advice, and wants to promote a working atmosphere where people feel comfortable expressing dissent. Second, he is also telling them that he welcomes debate as long as it is buttressed with empirical evidence and not just "arm-waving."

As noted earlier, most political appointees come into office possessing advanced degrees and substantial professional experience in government and the private sector. They have survived and thrived in professional life in part because they have learned to listen to their advisers before making a decision. No appointees want to make the wrong decision. Not only could such a decision have disastrous consequences for the agency they lead, but it could also spell the end of their political career. The White House wants its political appointees to pursue the "right" ideological agenda, but it also wants its people to be competent executives who run effective organizations.

Myth 4: Political appointees (historically Republicans) don't like government employees.

Many careerists initially assume that political appointees arrive in office with a disdainful attitude about the career staff. Since appointees, by definition, have not chosen to make government their full-time career, the assumption is that this must mean that appointees tend to hold very negative beliefs about career employees. And, at least since the administration of Richard Nixon, many careerists have tended to assume that Republican appointees, in particular, are antagonistic toward careerists. In part, this myth arises from the ideology of the Republican Party, which stresses smaller government and the advantages of "running government more like a business." It is natural for civil servants to assume that if Republicans are skeptical about bureaucracy, then they must also be skeptical about the bureaucrats themselves.

Table 3.7: Myths (and Realities) about Political Appointees

Myth	Reality
Political appointees care only about ideology and not about organizational stewardship.	• Most political appointees care about leaving the agency a better place than they found it and want to have a positive impact on the organization.
Political appointees are not really competent for their jobs.	• Political appointees are highly educated. • Many political appointees have worked in government before. • Many political appointees have worked in or with their specific agency before. • Many political appointees have expertise in policy-relevant subjects.
Political appointees do not want to hear information that contradicts their ideological agendas.	• Most political appointees want to make sound decisions based on facts. • Most political appointees are interested in "getting it right."
Political appointees (historically Republicans) don't like government employees.	• How smoothly the political/career relationship evolves rarely has anything to do with party affiliation. • Managerial and interpersonal factors are far more important.

Retellings of this myth also often point to the excesses of the Nixon administration, which of course was headed by Republicans. Some civil servants are old enough to remember the infamous "Malek Manual," in which Nixon's personnel director, Fred Malek, laid down various means for dealing with recalcitrant civil servants. And Nixon's federalism initiatives were widely seen as a way to weaken the federal bureaucracy by moving power and money from Washington to the states.

Our interviews suggest, however, that this belief is more myth than reality. Many of our career interviewees have served under both Republican and Democratic administrations, and their complaints—and compliments—about the political executives they have worked with transcend political party. We talked, for example, to careerists who identified themselves as lifelong Democrats who had spent their entire federal career working in social policy agencies—organizations that, according to the myth, are unpopular with Republicans. And yet many of these same career managers said that the most effective appointees they had worked with had been Republicans. For every careerist we interviewed who complained about Republicans not liking bureaucrats, there was another career official telling us a horror story about being unable to work with a Democrat who was "too ideological." Whether one is an effective political appointee seems to have little to do with political party; it is more about personal management style.

Rules of Engagement for Career Civil Servants

Based on our research, we offer some rules of engagement for career officials. We have tried to distill the collective wisdom of our interviewees, who among themselves have hundreds of years of experience working in the federal government and dealing with political executives. These rules are summarized in Table 3.8 on page 61.

Rule 1: Know your job and develop your expertise.

A clear conclusion from our interviews with appointees is that political executives value careerists more for their technical expertise than their political opinions. As a careerist, the more knowledgeable you are about the policy issues at hand, the more valuable you will be to the political leadership. Remember that a key role of the career civil servant is to speak truth to power. As a career employee, odds are that you probably know more about the relevant policy and the institutional history than the political executive you serve. Most political appointees understand this and want your advice and counsel. Like most executives, political appointees want to make good decisions, and part of making good decisions is getting good advice. That is where the technically proficient careerist comes in.

One political appointee told us, "You really need to trust the staff; otherwise you will drown." Another said, "The in-box can eat you alive. You have to trust and delegate to the staff." Effective political executives understand this and will be more likely to delegate substantial work to their careerists if they perceive the career staff to be on top of the policy and programmatic details.

One of our political interviewees said that in her view, the most effective careerists were those who were "comfortable with data and analysis, not just opinions and anecdotes," and were "willing to change their minds and their direction based on what the data were telling them." Other political appointees told us that the least effective careerists were people who "shoot from the hip" and are "anecdote based."

Rule 2: Understand (and embrace) your role.

Political appointees and careers play different roles in public administration. Political executives shape and deliver the policy message to the public, the media, and the Congress, while careerists work largely behind the scenes during the formulation and implementation stages of the policy process. Several political appointees we interviewed said that problems sometimes arose with their careerists because of role confusion.

One political appointee told a story about a careerist who decided that he would not only help craft a press release on an important policy initiative but that he should be the one to deliver it to the media. The appointee had to rebuke the career employee and explain that she, not he, was the person to play the role of public spokesperson. She went on to explain that this careerist was not a bad employee—indeed, she found him to be one of the most competent staffers on her team—but simply someone who had blundered into the wrong territory and was trying to do the job of the political leadership.

Of course, a strong and continuing sense of role confusion may be a sign that you, as a careerist, are in the wrong line of work. We also interviewed former career government employees who now work for political action committees or lobbying firms. These interviewees said that what drove them to leave government service was that they found themselves constantly longing to be more involved in policy decision making and advocacy; they did not feel content with their role as policy analysts and formulators. They came to the realization that they would be more effective (and happier) if they left government service and took on more political work. Similarly, many of our political appointees explained that they could not conceive of working for a leadership team whose ideology differed from theirs.

Rule 3: Be patient.

Anyone who has ever worked in government knows that change does not happen overnight. Sometimes it does not happen at all. A key to surviving in the bureaucracy, therefore, is to be patient. It is human nature to expect rapid change when a new leadership team enters office. Career civil servants are certainly prone to this expectation as the presidential election season gives way to the transition to governance. But patience is important. New political appointees need time to learn their way around the organization.

During the transition and (for Senate-confirmed officials) the preparation for their confirmation hearings, incoming political appointees will be bombarded with briefings about countless policies and programs. And, quite often, the list of issues that is "teed up" during the initial transition briefings does not necessarily become the working agenda once the administration settles in. So, part of patience is learning that it may take time before you even get an opportunity to present issues in your area to the new political team. But part of it is also knowing that an issue must "ripen" before a window of opportunity opens for meaningful action. Knowing the technical aspects of your policy is important, but so is staying aware of the political calendar.

Rule 4: Learn something about the new political leadership.

Many of our career interviewees recommended getting to know something about the new political leadership—well before the first face-to-face meeting. As soon as the presidential nomination is officially announced (or even before—it is not too difficult for a connected senior careerist to figure out who is on the short list), it makes sense to get a copy of the nominee's résumé. What is his or her most recent position? What is his area of expertise? Has she served in government before? Has she served in your agency before? Has he written books or articles or even editorials that might give you some sense of his policy positions or what he might advance as his key issue agenda?

Doing some research along these lines will help you in several ways. First, it gives you some sense of the person who is assuming a leadership position. Of course, even extensive background reading about the nominee does not guarantee a totally accurate picture, but it is probably better than approaching your new boss completely unaware of her background. Second, knowing something about the new political executive will help you more effectively market your policy ideas. Several of our career interviewees

Role Confusion: The Case of Former National Park Police Chief Teresa Chambers

In December 2003, the Department of the Interior placed National Park Police Chief Teresa Chambers on administrative leave because it alleged that she had discussed budget and staffing shortfalls with the media and improperly lobbied the Congress. Later, in July 2004, the department fired Chambers, a career employee and 27-year veteran of law enforcement. As this is written, Chambers has fought her dismissal in court and in the press, and has lost her latest attempt to be reinstated to her former position.[23]

On October 7, 2004, a federal administrative law judge from the Merit Systems Protection Board ruled that Chambers was not a whistleblower but rather a problem employee with a history of defying her superiors and ignoring established agency procedures. Among other things, the judge ruled that Chambers circumvented the official chain of command by directly approaching the deputy secretary of the Interior about an employee transfer.

What happened? Federal employee advocates see the Chambers case as a textbook illustration of heavy-handed political manipulation of the career bureaucracy. After she was initially put on administrative leave, for example, Congressman Steny Hoyer (D-Md.) praised Chambers for being honest and said he was worried that other government managers might be discouraged from speaking out because of the disciplinary actions taken against her. Of course, her superiors at Interior see it as an unfortunate situation brought on by an uncooperative career employee who overstepped her bounds.

Based on the research for this study, we might argue that the Chambers case is, in part, a cautionary tale for careerists. The moral of this tale is twofold. First, understand your role and know the boundaries of your position. Second, transgress those boundaries at your own peril. In speaking to the press about the budget and personnel problems at the Park Police, and in going around her chain of command to talk to the number two political executive at the department, Chambers was perceived as acting more like a political appointee herself than a career manager. In trying to agitate public opinion to influence the budget process for her agency, Chambers was perceived as moving from the realm of career manager to would-be political executive. Of course, Chambers is not the first career manager to take such actions, nor will she be the last, but her case illustrates the potential perils of role confusion.

---

described themselves as having the job of marketing ideas to the political leadership. Success is partly dependent on presenting an idea that is well-thought-out and thoroughly researched, but success is also dependent on knowing what will sell.

One interviewee told us about his experiences in proposing various efficiency initiatives. In this case, a new political appointee was very interested

---

What Political Appointees Said about Careerists

On Effective Career Civil Servants
"Comfortable operating with data—not just opinions and anecdotes."
"Ability to move between the big picture and the tiny details."
"Willing to change direction based on what the data shows."
"Smart, engaged, and analytical in their approach."
"Willing to step out front and take a risk."

On Ineffective Career Civil Servants
"They shoot from the hip—don't really have the data to back them up."
"Overprotective of their image—trying so hard to be 'neutral' that they don't really do the job."
"Did not understand that their job was not to present the message or speak to the media."
"Some of them were just too averse to risk."

Political Appointees' Advice to Career Civil Servants
"Realize that most political appointees are very interested in public service."
"If you come in with anecdotes not backed up with data and analysis, then you are not going to get very far."
"Remember that political appointees need to be responsive to the White House and the president's agenda."
"You may think that the answers don't often change, but when new political appointees come in, the questions definitely will change."

---

in such initiatives but also very much a proponent of competitive sourcing. Knowing this, the careerist made sure to incorporate contracting and outsourcing proposals into his overall efficiency presentation, and felt that it made a stronger impression on the political appointee.

Rule 5: Be aware of the bigger picture.

As a careerist, there is no question that you bring a lot of passion and enthusiasm to your area of policy expertise. But there is also no question that, on any given day, your political superiors are worried about many more issues than just yours. Moreover, political appointees may not simply look at your issue from your technical perspective, but may have to incorporate, and accommodate, a variety of other perspectives in the process of fashioning a political compromise. For you as the technically savvy career expert, the best answer is the "right" answer. For the political appointee, the best answer may likely be the "achievable" answer.

One political appointee we interviewed explained it this way: "I need to temper the career input with politics." Another political interviewee said, "Sometimes I may have to make a decision based on the politics that goes against the technical recommendation, no matter how sound that recommendation was." It is important to note here that these political executives are not talking about "politics" in its lowest, most narrow sense, as if making decisions "based on the politics" means brazenly ignoring good technical advice to perform a political favor for some interested party. Rather, what they mean is that the career technical input is one input among many—an

Table 3.8: Rules of Engagement for Career Civil Servants

Rule	Illustration
Know your job and develop your expertise.	• Be an expert in your policy area. • Give the political leadership high-quality analytical products.
Understand and embrace your role.	• Understand the role of the careerist in the American political system. • Take pride in your contributions to an effective policy process. • Avoid acting too "political."
Be patient.	• Avoid pushing too hard for action, particularly with new political leaders. • Understand that decisions cannot be made on all issues and that certain topics take priority.
Learn something about the new political leadership.	• Read their résumés. • Get to know something about their policy expertise and their positions on key issues. • Talk to people who have served with them in previous positions.
Be aware of the bigger picture.	• Realize that political appointees sometimes have to accommodate other perspectives, not just yours. • Understand that political appointees see their role as protecting the president and advancing his agenda. • Know what else is going on in your department and in your overall issue area.

important input, to be sure, particularly if it is rigorous and highly analytical, but still just one input that must be balanced against other considerations.

It is also important to note that many of our political interviewees stressed the importance of the president's interests. After all, as political appointees, they serve at the pleasure of the president and have been appointed to their positions in large part to fulfill the president's wishes and advance his policy agenda. One interviewee put it this way: "At the end of the day, I have to make decisions in the president's interest."

Rules of Engagement for Political Appointees

Political appointees in the federal government have a lot on their plates. They are often responsible for millions, if not billions, of taxpayers' dollars. They often manage programs or policy areas that affect thousands, if not millions, of lives. They often have supervisory responsibility for hundreds of federal employees. And they must worry about carrying out the public interest at the same time they focus on the issues that are important to critical political coalitions, interest groups, Congress, the press, and their boss (the president). Theirs is a complicated world. Managing the bureaucracy is perhaps the least of their worries, but if they can figure out how to do it well—to marshal the resources of the civil service—they will undoubtedly improve their chances of success.

Along with soliciting opinions about the misconceptions that political appointees had about careerists, we also asked careerists to tell us what successful appointees did that worked well. Conversely, we also asked them to characterize not-so-successful appointees. Since most careerists had extensive experience working with different appointees through numerous administrations, many were able to see patterns in terms of what works and what doesn't work in Washington. Based on these interviews, we developed the following "rules of engagement." The rules are summarized in Table 3.9 on page 69.

Rule 1: Engage the career staff and listen to their advice—even if you don't heed it.

Most careerists understand that their advice cannot always be followed. In cases where it is not, one political appointee told us that he often had information (and pressures) that the careerists did not know about. As a result, he knew that careerists would not like some of the decisions that he made, but he felt compelled to make them anyway. Although appointees may not always be able to share sensitive information about the foundation for their decisions, oftentimes having a hearing is enough to satisfy careerists that they are contributing to the process and that they add value. Feeling as if they've been heard encourages them to give appointees important information and advice the next time.

In chapter two on what successful appointees do, Judith Michaels also stressed "turning to career staff." There are many reasons for doing this—tapping their expertise and experience, delegating workload, ensuring that there is buy-in during implementation—but the issue we found careerists focusing on was related to management and motivation. That is, careerists want to feel like they are contributing to the mission of their organizations. If political managers cut them out of processes or if their advice is rarely sought, they suffer from a sort of professional identity crisis. Such an identity crisis negatively affects their job satisfaction and motivation. Ultimately, the productivity and the effectiveness of the organization will be negatively affected, too.

Careerists are the institutional memory of American public administration. As noted earlier, they draw the policy maps that connect the past, present, and future. They are the keepers of the institutional "lore" and can tell political appointees the stories that explain what has and hasn't worked before. As Richard Neustadt once wrote, "What makes lore invaluable is the sad fact that no institutional sources of memory exist as substitutes, save patchily, by happenstance, at higher executive levels of American government. Lore is almost all there is. Without it, available documentation tends to be ambiguous, misleading, or perverse."[24]

Rule 2: Show the career staff that you respect them.

Several careerists mentioned that political appointees don't tend to understand or appreciate the resources they have at their disposal. It would save many false starts if appointees read their new staff's résumés. Knowing the expertise and skills of the career staff helps appointees effectively use those resources. Also, given career executives' relatively long tenure in their organizations, they tend to know what the organization's management issues are and what the internal politics are. Careerists are anxious to team up with appointees to improve management. Less successful appointees paid little attention to the staff resources they had; more successful appointees harnessed staff resources effectively. And in order to harness the resources, you need to know what resources are at your disposal.

According to our career interviewees, the best appointees are also good managers. While careerists understand that appointees have a political mission they are trying to accomplish, appointees are also usually expected to

Not Listening to Careerists: The Case of Thomas Scully, Richard Foster, and the Medicare Program

While the Teresa Chambers case offers an example of a career manager over-stepping her bounds and acting too "political," the case of Richard Foster, chief actuary of the Medicare program, shows how political appointees can run into trouble when they do not listen to their career technical experts.[25]

During the development of the president's budget for Fiscal Year 2005, one of Foster's key responsibilities was to estimate the costs of the administration's proposed new Medicare prescription-drug bill under consideration at that time by the Congress. While the Congressional Budget Office (CBO) had estimated that the new program would cost about $395 billion, Foster's internal estimate was much higher, nearly $534 billion. President Bush was having trouble convincing conservatives to support the program, and many of these legislators said they would only endorse the bill as long as the total price tag did not exceed $400 billion. While legislators naturally had access to the CBO estimate, some members were asking the Department of Health and Human Services to release their internal estimates as well. But these requests were denied.

Congress voted for passage of the president's program but later became aware of Foster's higher estimates. In testimony before Congress in March 2004, Foster alleged that Thomas Scully, former head of the Centers for Medicare & Medicaid Services, had threatened to fire him if he responded to congressional requests for his cost estimates. According to Foster, he reminded Scully that the language in the 1997 Budget Act that created the actuary position called for an independent office charged with providing Congress prompt and impartial information. Scully dismissed this argument.

What happened in this case? The White House argues that Scully was acting unilaterally and without administration guidance in suppressing Foster's cost estimates. Foster, in his testimony before Congress and various media interviews, has said that Scully was in fact suppressing his estimates.

Based on our research, we would argue that this case shows the risks that political appointees run when they fail to trust their career staffs and, worse, actively work to suppress their analyses. Unlike Teresa Chambers, Foster did not circumvent his chain of command, even though he was clearly uncomfortable with being ordered not to respond to congressional requests. He did what a good career civil servant is supposed to do: He spoke truth to power. But in this case, power did not listen. Some might say that it would have been politically inept to release the internal estimates to Congress, given the fact that conservative members were openly complaining about the price tag. But it is entirely possible—and plausible—that had Foster been permitted to share his numbers with Congress, the bill would still have passed. House Ways and Means Committee Chairman Bill Thomas, for instance, said in interviews at the time that he supported Foster and that his estimates were just that—estimates. "I support you now," said Thomas. "It does not mean that I'm going to agree with your estimates." In other words, Thomas, an influential committee chair, would not have seen Foster's estimates as the death knell for the proposed bill but rather as just another set of estimates. Suppressing Foster's analyses may have paid some short-term political benefits, but at the longer-term cost of sparking a nasty dispute with Congress and demeaning the role career experts play in bringing forth technical advice to policy makers.

manage various components of an agency or department. Successful appointees tend to manage by walking around and making an effort to inject fun into the work. Those who were characterized as ineffective or "making critical mistakes" were abusive and rude to subordinates. One focus group participant characterized one appointee he worked for as "tyrannical and intimidating."

Two career interviewees offered vivid portraits of these different management styles. On the positive side, one interviewee told us about the deputy secretary of his department who would often eat lunch in the employee cafeteria. "It was like he was saying that I am on your team. I am no better than you." At first, career employees noticed the deputy secretary going through the lunch line but did not feel comfortable approaching him; after a while, though, it became common for careerists to take their lunch trays over to the deputy's table and join him for lunch.

Another career interviewee painted a darker picture. This person worked for an assistant secretary who was often rude and dismissive of others' opinions. Rather than an opportunity for information exchange, staff meetings became ordeals to be survived. At briefings, the assistant secretary would seemingly go out of his way to exhibit disinterest in the information and recommendations being presented. At one such briefing, our interviewee told us that the assistant secretary actually rose from his seat, strode to the front of the room, and unceremoniously flicked off the overhead projector that a senior career employee was using to present transparencies. Needless to say, this is not a management style that will win over the career staff.

Rule 3: Be willing to be educated about the programs and policies.

Even the most well-seasoned appointees can't know the program and policy detail (and history) as well as a lot of careerists. Careerists are anxious to teach appointees about the important issues in their programs. Take advantage of being new on the job by asking a lot of questions and soliciting information from the career staff. Appointees who learned their programs were more able to take action when they needed to, according to career

What Careerists Said about Political Appointees

On Effective Political Appointees
"Considered analysis when making decisions."
"Was a rational decision maker."
"Knew how to delegate."
"Got to know the career staff."
"Treated people decently and with respect."
"Had good relationships with the White House and Capitol Hill."
"Involved me in high-level meetings."
"Consistent and honest."
"Willing to find out what programs and strategies have worked in the past."
"Did not assume the career staff was wedded to the prior administration."

On Ineffective Political Appointees
"Never developed a real working relationship with the career staff."
"Did not have a specific, doable action agenda."
"Never really knew what they wanted to accomplish."
"Just refused to compromise."
"Insecure, and afraid to make decisions."
"Abusive and rude to people."
"Managed by intimidation."
"Unwilling to say, 'I made a mistake.' "
"Too focused on a narrow political agenda."

Careerists' Advice to Political Appointees
"Most civil servants want to help."
"Realize that it will take time to implement the administration's agenda."
"Make sure to give the career staff good feedback—let them know what happens at the big meetings."
"You have to trust the staff—you cannot do everything by yourself."

executives. Lack of program knowledge also fosters a lack of confidence in some appointees, which makes them less effective bargainers within the organization.

Careerists also pointed to the importance of context in decision making. Careerists are in a unique position to provide most political appointees with the historical, legal, and organizational context they need to understand complicated policy and program issues. Appointees who "did not listen" to this context were more likely to fail, according to career executives, because the proverbial devil is often in the details.

Rule 4: Have a clear and limited set of objectives.

Successful presidents are known for having clear and limited agendas. Similarly, appointees need to have clear and limited objectives if they expect staff to focus their energies appropriately. Careerists want to understand the priorities of an appointee. When they don't know the agenda, careerists feel as if they're operating in the dark: playing a guessing game about what the appointee expects from them and perhaps directing their attention to the wrong priorities. Of course, the appointee must *develop* clear and limited objectives. This is the threshold issue. One interviewee said that "governing is more of a focus on principles than politics." What she means is that once the election campaign is over, political appointees must choose priorities and make hard decisions. To be successful, political executives have to be careful to set goals that are ambitious, but not so lofty that they end up being unachievable.

Rule 5: Be willing to compromise on your agenda and admit mistakes.

Successful appointees are pragmatic about the need to compromise. In our interviews, careerists argued that appointees who dug in their heels on every issue ended up achieving none of their agenda. Although careerists are not always privy to the political issues appointees face during decision making, they can often provide expertise, advice, and workable alternatives in the face of failing initiatives. Careerists are anxious to provide this kind of service to political appointees.

Mid-course corrections are inevitable during the policy-making process. Careerists expect political appointees to make mistakes like everyone else. Ill will is created when appointees refuse to admit mistakes—or, worse yet, when they blame mistakes on career staff. According to the careerists we talked to, they have the most respect for managers who take personal responsibility for their mistakes and are willing to make necessary changes to their agendas.

Rule 6: Don't forget about the organization.

Political appointees have a lot to worry about on any given day, but they must remember that they are also stewards, albeit for a limited amount of time, of the agencies they lead. Successful appointees understand that being serious about organizational stewardship pays dividends in several ways. It shows the career staff that you care about more than just achieving short-term policy goals. And leaving the organization in better shape than you found it is a real service to the American taxpayer.

How can political appointees be good organizational stewards? Our political interviewees shared several ideas. One strategy is to be willing to take on bureaucratic roadblocks and perform bureaucratic "miracles." One appointee told us about her experience in taking on a long-festering regulatory problem within her agency. Prior administrations had not been able to get a particular regulation through the clearance process; in recent years, many of the career staffers had lost interest, figuring it was an impossible task. But some senior careerists still saw this regulation as important. The appointee decided to take it on and make it one of her top priorities; eventually, her dedication paid off and the regulation was approved. By doing this, she not only had solved an administrative problem but also had won the respect and trust of the career staff.

Paying attention to human capital issues is another way to invest in organizational stewardship. One of our political interviewees, for example, told us that he tries to focus his attention at both ends of the human resources life cycle. At one end, he makes a point of attending new employee orientation events and job fairs. In his view, this sends a powerful message not only to the new employees and interns but also to the career staff that as a political executive, he is interested in more than just promoting new policies. At the other end of the spectrum, our interviewee said that he invests time in the overall workforce planning of the agency and has not shied away from dealing with thorny personnel issues, including making a serious effort to hold people accountable for their performance. This includes both rewarding high performers with choice assignments, awards, and promotions, as well as taking tough action when warranted for those who are not performing adequately.

Rule 7: Communicate, communicate, communicate.

Frequent and substantive communication between careerists and political appointees is the key to a productive working relationship. Although political appointees have severely limited time, communicating with career staff improves efficiency in the long run. For example, communicating the agenda, objectives, and priorities allows career managers and staff to direct their resources appropriately. Communicating expectations of the career staff—how appointees see them contributing to the stated objectives—gives careerists a sense of direction and a sense that they are partners in the process. Providing consistent performance feedback allows careerists to provide the kind of service and information that is most useful to an appointee. In summary, frequent communication is an important key to good management. Good management makes the workforce more productive and more motivated and, in the end, makes for better government.

Table 3.9: Rules of Engagement for Political Appointees

Rule	Illustration
Engage the career staff and listen to their advice—even if you don't heed it.	• Involve the career staff in agency deliberations. • Actively solicit their analysis and recommendations.
Show the career staff that you respect them.	• Read your careerists' résumés. • Understand their skills and what they bring to the table. • Make it clear that you are the decision maker, but treat them as a partner.
Spend some time learning the details.	• Ask lots of questions—particularly as you enter office. • Find out why some initiatives have worked and others haven't. • Knowing the details gives you stronger credibility within the agency and improves your chances of achieving your agenda.
Have a clear and limited set of objectives.	• Motivate the career staff with ambitious but achievable objectives. • Make sure the careerists know where you're going. • Make sure *you* know where you're going.
Be willing to compromise and admit mistakes.	• Realize that sometimes you have to give a little to gain a little. • Be strong but pragmatic. • Take responsibility for your mistakes.
Don't forget about the organization.	• Pay attention to organizational stewardship. • Take on bureaucratic and administrative problems within the agency. • Make an effort to attend job fairs and new employee orientation events. • Don't shy away from tough human resource management issues.
Communicate, communicate, communicate.	• Constantly communicate your goals. • Constantly give the career staff feedback about ongoing agency deliberations. • Make sure that the staff understands why decisions have been made the way they were. • Give the staff feedback on their performance.

Findings and Recommendations

Both political appointees and career civil servants are critical to the success of any president's agenda. Working together, these two groups are responsible for executing and maintaining the federal government's myriad programs. These programs touch millions of lives. If relationships between political appointees and careerists are strained, their work naturally suffers. If their work suffers, the American people are not well served. Thus, our contention is that the quality of American governance is highly dependent on the ability of political appointees and careerists in the executive branch to work well together—by understanding and honoring each other's perspectives; by committing themselves to good management in the organizations of which they are a part; and by communicating with each other about roles, priorities, and objectives.

In this chapter, we provided lists of myths that can undermine a positive start to the political/career relationship. We also offered some rules of engagement for both groups. Here we provide our main findings, with related recommendations for establishing and maintaining effective working relationships in the future.

Finding 1: Myths are counterproductive.

- Myths about both political appointees and careerists are powerful, but they are based on exceptions rather than rules.
- Myths drive counterproductive behavior like distrust and secrecy.
- Myth-based beliefs inhibit communication between political appointees and careerists.

Recommendations

Having preconceived notions about anyone is not only unfair, it is also counterproductive to forging a productive working relationship. Suspend your suspicion and your belief in myths until you get to know each other. Assume the best until proven otherwise. Research shows that when political appointees and careerists settle into a working relationship, they usually have a very positive view of each other. Contrary to the well-worn proverb, when it comes to political appointees and careerists, familiarity breeds respect, not contempt. Given this, we recommend skipping right to the respect and forgoing the potentially myth-laden "getting to know you" phase.

Finding 2: Good management is important, and lacking.

- Both political and career executives care about good management, but both groups are critical of each other on this score.
- Both political and career executives want to partner on management issues, but that doesn't happen very often.
- Careerists want political appointees to be leaders; political appointees want careerists to show them the management ropes.
- Political appointees have a shorter-term perspective than careerists, but both groups care about the long-term health of the organizations for which they work.

Recommendations

Management should be an explicit priority and should be a team effort between careerists and political appointees. Collaboration should start with specifically defining management roles, setting management objectives, and talking about management philosophy (bearing in mind that actions will ultimately speak a lot louder than words). Political appointees should rely on the specific assets of career executives—for example, knowledge of the organizational politics and experience with the federal personnel rules. Careerists should rely on the expertise and experience political appointees bring from managing other organizations. Both groups should view themselves as organizational stewards, even as their time horizons are quite different.

Finding 3: Cultural clashes are inevitable but not fatal.

- Careerists tend to arrive at their positions through a system that values expertise, experience, and technical ability. They care about fair and open processes and the "means" through which things get done.
- Political appointees behave more like entrepreneurs, valuing innovation and quick action. The entrepreneur cares about the kind of change that is being made, or the "ends" of what gets done.
- Political appointees and careerists both value public service, but they define it differently. Careerists are there to do the nation's business; political appointees are there to determine what the nation's business should be.

Recommendations

Means and ends are both important to the American system of government. The ends represent the "what" (the substance) of public administration and the means represent the "how" (the process). The substance of public administration has its roots in electoral legitimacy, bestowed on each administration by the American people. But if substantive change is formulated or implemented without fair processes, it will not be considered legitimate.

The different perspectives of careerists and political appointees derive, in part, from the different systems in which they have matured. These systems define their roles, and role perceptions drive behavior. Both roles are critical, but they are also clearly different. The differences can only be reconciled by acknowledging their existence. Political appointees and careerists should make an effort to understand and respect the other's contribution to our system of government. Problems arise when one group misunderstands its role, usurps the other's role, or shuts the other out of decision making.

Finding 4: Communication is the key to success.

- Suspicion and distrust inhibit communication and learning.
- Unclear or unlimited goals, objectives, and priorities set the organization up for failure.
- Speaking truth to power serves everyone well.

Recommendations

Suspending preconceived notions facilitates more open communication, which is essential in forging a productive working relationship between careerists and political appointees. Each should make a concerted effort to get to know each other: Political appointees should read staff résumés so they know what skills and abilities the careerists bring to the work; careerists should learn about appointees' backgrounds so they can focus their efforts on filling in substantive gaps. Political appointees should communicate their goals, objectives, and priorities early and often. Similarly, political appointees should give careerists frequent performance feedback so mid-course corrections can be made.

Finally, we recommend that careerists continue (or start, if they don't already) to challenge political appointees' assumptions and hypotheses. This kind of dialogue is critical to good decision making, it personifies the role of the civil service, and most political appointees value the input.

Acknowledgments

We would like to thank Mark Abramson and Jonathan Breul of the IBM Center for The Business of Government for their support and assistance during this project. Their comments and suggestions were very useful in helping us develop our approach to this project.

And, of course, we would like to thank the political appointees and career civil servants who agreed to spend some of their valuable time, sharing with us their insights and reflections about government service. To the extent that this chapter contains any wisdom for future officeholders, career or political, it is the wisdom of the people we interviewed.

Appendix: Study Methodology

Our methodology focused on three main tasks:
- Reviewing the relevant scholarly literature.
- Conducting focus groups and personal interviews with appointees and high-level careerists.
- Synthesizing lessons learned from political appointees who manage or who have managed within the civil service (primary and secondary sources).

Literature Review

We reviewed several theoretical and empirical studies by academics and government agencies. The academic literature focused on bureaucratic politics, public administration, public policy, and management. Government reports focused on demographics and employee attitudes. All sources are cited within the chapter, and a complete list can be found in the bibliography.

Focus Groups

We conducted two focus groups—one with current and former political appointees (six participants) and a second consisting of current and former career executives (eight participants). Although data gathered from this methodology are not generalizable, there are important advantages to using this methodology. First, it allows researchers to gather many opinions at one time. Second, because of the conversational atmosphere, it sparks ideas and thoughts among participants that they may not have had in a one-on-one interview. And third, it fosters group synergy—the whole is greater than the sum of its parts. The technique used was based on Richard Kreuger's method of conducting focus groups and the questioning routes used are provided in Table 3.A.1.

Interviews

We conducted 12 in-depth interviews with current and former political appointees, 25 with current and former career executives, and three with people who had served in both capacities. Like focus group data, data from interviews are not generalizable. What they offer are interesting illustrations, texture, and rich description based on the research questions. The questionnaires used during the in-depth interviews are provided in Table 3.A.2 on pages 76–77.

Lessons Learned

Using a combination of the information from the literature, the focus groups, and the in-depth interviews, we developed lessons learned and summarized them by category.

Table 3.A.1: Questions Used in Focus Groups

Questioning Route— Careerist Focus Group	Questioning Route— Political Appointee Focus Group
Think back to the transitions between various administrations you've worked through in your federal career. How would you describe most of the appointees who came in to fill political slots?	Think back to when you first started working as a political appointee in the federal government. What were your first impressions of the career civil servants who worked for you?
How would you describe the relationship between careerists and political appointees?	How did your impressions change (if they changed) over the course of your tenure, and what caused those impressions to change?
What are the key factors in determining the character of that relationship?	How would you describe the relationship between careerists and political appointees?
When you think about effective political appointees, what actions did they take that made them successful in your eyes?	What are the key factors in determining the character of that relationship?
What about political appointees who weren't so effective? What critical mistakes did they make?	When you think about effective careerists, what kinds of things do they do that make them successful in your eyes?
What should political appointees know about the career civil service before they start working in the federal government?	What about careerists who aren't so effective? What critical mistakes do they make?
What specific misconceptions do you think political appointees tend to have about the career civil service?	What specific misconceptions do you think careerists have about political appointees?
What specific misconceptions do you think careerists have about political appointees?	What specific misconceptions do you think political appointees have about careerists?

Table 3.A.2: Questions Used in Interviews

Interview Questions for Careerists	Interview Questions for Political Appointees
During transitions between administrations, how would you describe your first impressions of most of the appointees who came in to fill political slots?	When you first began working as a political appointee, what were your first impressions of the career civil servants who worked for you?
Did your impressions of them tend to change over time? If so, how?	How did your impressions change (if they changed) over the course of your tenure?
What caused those impressions to change (if yes to question 2)?	What caused those impressions to change (if yes to question 2)?
How would you describe the relationship between careerists and political appointees generally?	Given your experience, how would you describe the relationship between careerists and political appointees in general in the federal government?
What are the key factors in determining the character of that relationship?	What are the key factors in determining the character of that relationship?
When you think about effective political appointees, what actions did they take that made them successful in your eyes?	What are the major misunderstandings between career civil servants and political appointees?
What about political appointees who weren't so effective? What critical mistakes did they make?	When you think about effective careerists, what kinds of things do they do that make them successful in your eyes?
What should political appointees know about the career civil service before they start working in the federal government?	What about careerists who aren't so effective? What critical mistakes do they make?

What specific misconceptions do you think political appointees tend to have about the career civil service at the beginning of their working relationship? What are the misconceptions they continue to have even after they work with civil servants?	What specific misconceptions do you think political appointees tend to have about the career civil service at the beginning of their working relationship? What are the misconceptions they continue to have even after they work with civil servants?
What specific misconceptions do you think careerists have about political appointees at the beginning of their working relationship? What are the misconceptions they continue to have even after they work with political appointees?	What specific misconceptions do you think careerists have about political appointees at the beginning of their working relationship? What are the misconceptions they continue to have even after they work with political appointees?
Given the topic of our research, are there other critical points that you'd like to make? Are there issues we've neglected? Are there other people you would recommend that we talk to?	Given the topic of our research, are there other critical points that you'd like to make? Are there issues we've neglected? Are there other people you would recommend that we talk to?

Endnotes

1. In this chapter, we use the terms *political executives, political appointees, politicals,* and *presidential appointees* interchangeably. A more detailed summary of the various categories of political executives is provided in Table 3.2.

2. The GAO calculated this figure by examining the tenure of all federal government political executives appointed after October 1, 1989, who left office before September 30, 2001. Other chapters have put the average tenure at about 24 months. See, for example, "Strengthening Senior Leadership in the Federal Government," the report of a National Academy of Public Administration panel issued in December 2002.

3. In this chapter we use the terms *career government employees, careerists, careers,* and *civil servants* interchangeably.

4. It should be noted that career government employees includes not just civilian federal employees but also military personnel. However, this chapter does not attempt to address the special case of the military but rather focuses on career civilian executives.

5. Senior management being defined here as General Schedule 14–15.

6. These figures are drawn from the Office of Personnel Management website, which includes several sections describing the demographics of the federal workforce. See, for example, http://opm.gov/feddata/demograp/table1-5.pdf.

7. The numbers in this paragraph refer specifically to members of the career SES.

8. Occasionally there are exceptions when prominent members of the opposition party are appointed to a high position within the president's administration; recent examples are Republican Bill Cohen's appointment to be Secretary of Defense in the Democratic Clinton administration and Democrat Norman Mineta's appointment to be Secretary of Transportation in the Republican George W. Bush administration.

9. See Stone, especially chapter 6.

10. These data come from the Office of Personnel Management workforce summaries.

11. See Mackenzie, 1987, and Aberbach and Rockman, 2000.

12. Or "two-on-one" sessions, when we were both present at an interview.

13. To promote candid and open discussions, we promised not to identify any of our interviewees by name or organizational affiliation.

14. Jones, pp. 167–68.

15. The 20th Amendment to the Constitution (1934) eliminated the lame-duck session of Congress, which previously met from December to March 3rd, the day before the new president was sworn in. Now the new Congress meets on January 3rd, 17 days before the swearing in, which is now specified as January 20th of the year after the election. The effects of this change were not felt until Eisenhower was elected in 1952 because FDR and Truman were both Democrats. Every change of president since that time has been a change of party except the George H. W. Bush administration in 1989.

16. Jones, p. 167.

17. Aberbach and Rockman, 2000, refer to the guild versus entrepreneurial systems to describe the differences in career paths between civil service executives and political appointees. This description aptly reflects some of the differences in motivation and performance on the job between the two groups, and is consistent with our findings.

18. It should be noted that, as with all these myths, there are small kernels of truth that help give the myths their staying power. In this case, it is true that many political appointees have in fact contributed money to the candidate's campaign. The Presidential Appointee Initiative at the Brookings Institution found in a 2001 study of Clinton and George W. Bush appointees that more than half of the 640 politicals they studied contributed money to the campaigns of the president who later appointed them.

19. See especially Aberbach and Rockman.

20. See Mackenzie, chapter 1.

21. See, for example, Mackenzie, chapter 1.

22. See, for example, Mackenzie, chapter 1.

23. There have been numerous articles on this subject. See, for example, David A. Fahrenthold, "Hoyer Calls for Return of Police Chief," *The Washington Post,* December 11, 2003, p. B-05; and Henri E. Cauvin, "Judge Lambastes Park Police Ex-Chief," *The Washington Post,* October 9, 2004, p. B-01.

24. Richard Neustadt in Jones, p. 167.

25. There have also been numerous articles about the Foster case, including Emily Heil, "Medicare Actuary Details Threats Over Estimates," *Government Executive Magazine,* March 25, 2004 (see www.govexec.com); and Amy Goldstein, "Foster: White House Had Role in Withholding Data," *The Washington Post,* March 19, 2004, p. A02.

Bibliography

Aberbach, Joel, and Bert Rockman. 2000. *In The Web of Politics: Three Decades of the Federal Executive.* Washington, D.C.: Brookings Institution Press.

Abramson, Mark, Steven Clyburn, and Elizabeth Mercier. 1999. "Results of the Government Leadership Survey: A 1999 Survey of Federal Executives." Washington, D.C.: IBM Center for The Business of Government.

Cauvin, Henri E. "Judge Lambastes Park Police Ex-Chief," *The Washington Post,* October 9, 2004, p. B-01.

Fahrenthold, David A. "Hoyer Calls for Return of Police Chief," *The Washington Post,* December 11, 2003, p. B-05.

Goldstein, Amy. "Foster: White House Had Role in Withholding Data," *The Washington Post,* March 19, 2004, p. A02.

Government Accountability Office. 2003. *Strategic Human Capital Management* (GAO Report 03-120). Washington, D.C.

Heil, Emily. "Medicare Actuary Details Threats Over Estimates," *Government Executive Magazine,* March 25, 2004 (see www.govexec.com).

Jones, Charles O., editor. 2000. *Preparing to be President: The Memos of Richard E. Neustadt.* Washington, D.C.: AEI Press.

Krueger, Richard. 1990. *Focus Groups: A Practical Guide for Applied Research.* London: Sage Publications.

Mackenzie, G. Calvin, editor. 1987. *The In-and-Outers: Presidential Appointees* and *Transient Government in Washington.* Baltimore, Md.: The Johns Hopkins University Press.

Michaels, Judith E. 2005. "Becoming an Effective Political Executive: 7 Lessons from Experienced Appointees" (2nd ed.) Washington, D.C.: IBM Center for The Business of Government.

National Academy of Public Administration. 2002. "Strengthening Senior Leadership in the Federal Government," December 2002.

Rosen, Bernard. 1998. *Holding Government Bureaucracies Accountable* (3rd ed.) Westport, Conn.: Praeger Publishers.

Stone, Deborah. 2002. *Policy Paradox: The Art of Political Decision Making.* New York: W.W. Norton.

U.S. Office of Personnel Management, *Fed Fact Book 2003.* http://opm.gov/feddata/demograp/table1-5.pdf (accessed 10/25/04).

Van Riper, Paul. 1958. *History of the United States Civil Service.* Evanston, Ill.: Row, Peterson.

PART II

Working with Congress and the Media

CHAPTER FOUR

Working with the Congress

John H. Trattner
Senior Writer and Editor
Council for Excellence in Government

*This essay was originally published as part of "Becoming an Effective
Political Executive: 7 Lessons from Experienced Appointees"
in January 2001, with a second edition in January 2005.*

Working with the Congress

(The italicized quotes below are drawn from interviews of presidential appoin-
tees for **The 2000 Prune Book** *by John H. Trattner (Washington, D.C.: Council*
for Excellence in Government and the Brookings Institution Press, 2000) and
from panelists who took part in orientation conferences for new appointees
conducted by The Council and the White House from 1997 to 1999.)

If you're a presidential appointee who deals regularly with the Congress,
you may already recognize some of the striking contrasts, obvious and not
so obvious, between the Hill and your own branch of government.

Unlike the executive branch, with defined, stated objectives set by its
political leadership, the Congress is an arena where two parties push legislative agendas that are often in direct, open conflict. Further, a political party
running the executive branch normally has no problem controlling it or getting its various elements to pull in the same general direction. In the Congress, however, neither party—whether in the majority or minority—can
always count on such order within its ranks.

A majority's ability to control the decision on a given bill may only
be nominal.

The congressional operating schedule offers another useful comparison. Increasingly hostage to the demands of fund-raising and fence mend-
ing, the Congress's work on substance is nowhere near as orderly, nor its
progress as straight-line, as that of the executive branch. Its irregular pace
and rhythm, its fractionated processes, can skew the timing and legislative
hopes of any administration.

The Congress is now basically a Tuesday-to-Thursday club. What you
have is a lot of members of the House and Senate who come in Tuesday
morning, leave Thursday night, and are not here a lot.

Over time, such factors have widened the inherent differences in
approach and attitude between the two branches. That makes it harder for
people in either place to understand, and allow for, the work habits, tactics,
strategy, and outlook typical of the other. It's true as much for relationships
between career staffs as between executive branch appointees and members of Congress. How well you can manage across these divides has a lot to
do with the impact you can make in your job—how far you can go toward
your objectives.

A Few Critical Generalities

You shouldn't plunge into the congressional dimension of your job
without some overall appreciation of the Congress as probably the strongest,
certainly the most contentious, power center in a city with several of them.

A sense of this emerges from several comments by veteran observers, first about the job of the Congress:

The framers really had in mind making Congress a formidable power, the first branch of government, giving it powers to legislate, appropriate, investigate; giving them their own single constituencies to pay attention to; terms of office distinct from the president; a bicameral legislature that ensures substantial conflict between the House and the Senate—a natural tension that develops between politicians' need to represent their constituents and to engage in serious deliberation and policy making. It's a body remarkable for its division of labor and specialization and the importance of congressional staff. Remember the framers had in mind to make it a complex, personal, explicitly political process.

The source of its prerogative:

Article I of the Constitution is the Congress. It is not the executive branch, it is not the judicial branch, it is the Congress. The founding fathers felt that was the seminal force for democracy—where the people had the direct authority to influence their lives in a pluralistic system. The fact is, regardless of what we think about individual members, everything emanates from that source of power.

Its personality:

People from Will Rogers on have tried to diagnose and explain Congress. Some see it as an august deliberative body. One woman member of the House of Representatives referred to it as an unruly day-care center. Let me suggest another option: It suffers from attention deficit disorder.

The way it operates:

Simple majorities don't matter anymore. You either have unanimous consent to get something done, or you need a committed super majority of 60 or more. That puts a big burden on anybody doing business from the White House or from the agencies—the burden either to build unanimous consent for your issue or to activate a very committed super majority. The power the Constitution gives to the minority is still very evident. There are continued attempts to take away that power, but it's still a very important one in that it protects the minority.

Its members' sense of independence within their own parties:

People in the executive branch make the mistake, in terms of what they expect of the Congress, to assume that members of their own party there are supposed to carry out the president's will. Supposed to be the floor leaders for the president, supposed to be the point men and women for the president's programs. It is important to remember that members of Congress, even of your party, are only loosely part of the same team. And the reason is that they are part of a separate branch of government that takes its role as a separate branch of government very seriously.

Nor can you expect to work well with the Hill without mastering at least a few other fundamentals. It helps to know something about the House and Senate rules and about parliamentary procedures. It's almost mandatory to be familiar with structure and function—especially in the design and funding of executive branch programs.

On that front, a senior White House staffer with congressional experience recommends that appointees "know the difference between the appropriations and authorization committees." That may sound pretty elementary. But "those are different processes on the Hill that people sometimes don't distinguish from each other."

Decisions on Money and Programs

So let's look at that for a minute. According to House and Senate rules, here's basically how the Congress is supposed to provide money for government programs. The power to authorize funds belongs to legislative committees that have jurisdiction over the various areas of government responsibility—health, labor, science, defense, and so on—and over executive branch agencies and programs in those areas. They are the authorizing committees. The power actually to make the money available resides with the appropriations committees and their various subcommittees. As they move toward these decisions, committees conduct hearings where executive branch agency leaders or senior political managers make their case for the new or existing programs and money requests laid out in the president's annual budget message to the Congress.

Each year, the Congress divides its funding task into 13 regular money bills that cover all government agencies and functions (plus the District of Columbia). The rules prescribe an annual two-step procedure. In step one, an authorizing committee enacts a measure that can create, continue, or modify a program (or an agency) for a set or indefinite amount of time and approve the appropriation of money for it. The measure may specify the duties and functions of the program, its structure, and the responsibilities of the executive branch officials involved.

In step two, the appropriations committees, after getting the recommendations of their 13 subcommittees, allocate funds to the programs that have been authorized. These decisions then come to the floor of each house for approval. Differences between House and Senate versions of these decisions go to joint conference committees for resolution; the results of that go back to each floor for approval. Once that is in hand—and the president signs the measure—the programs or agencies affected finally have budget authority to incur obligations and spend the money. If unanticipated needs arise within a program during the fiscal year, the Congress can and often does provide supplemental funding in a separate measure.

Keep firmly in mind that there are two kinds of spending for federal programs—discretionary and direct. Generally, discretionary funding takes the two-step route outlined above. But direct spending is funded by the authorizing process alone and today accounts for about two-thirds of all outlays. Most direct spending goes into entitlement programs where the level of funding is already fixed by previously enacted law. Social Security, for example, gets its funding through permanent appropriations in the program's authorizing law. Other direct spending, like that for Medicaid, is an "appropriated entitlement"; it is funded each year by the appropriations committees, but the authorizing legislation controls the amount.

Those are the rules. How do they work in practice? As individual appropriations, the 13 money bills are supposed to go through the painstaking process outlined above and be adopted by October 1, the beginning of the fiscal year in which they apply. These years, it rarely happens. The reality is that only a handful of bills might get through on time. The Congress, with the deadline looming, hastily wraps the rest into one large "omnibus" bill for quick passage, which critics say is also largely unexamined passage. For any bills that still don't make it, legislators must enact what is called a continuing resolution. This makes stop-gap funding available for the affected agencies and programs until the appropriations can be made. (Sometimes agencies have gone through an entire fiscal year on continuing resolutions.) In cases of extensive deadlock, where agreement on most appropriations is still absent at the October 1 mark, the Congress has been known simply to stop the clock, postponing the deadline for a few days.

Appropriators Vs. Authorizers

Further, many observers believe the whip hand in making funding decisions for executive branch agencies increasingly belongs to the appropriators.

There are three political parties in Washington: the Republicans, the Democrats and the appropriators. And the appropriators operate at a different beat from everybody else.

"My own experience," says a political consultant with a lot of it, "is that the appropriations committees are quickly becoming the only committees in the sense that more and more stuff is getting done at the last minute." That refers to the habit in both Houses over the last decade or more to put off most individual funding for agencies or groups of agencies during a legislative session, then fold them all into monster "omnibus" bills enacted in the last few days. As this individual points out, "the number of what would ordinarily be called authorizing pieces of legislation that are rolled into the omnibus bills is quite long."

"The authorizers do have a lot of impact on appropriations committee language," adds a former congressman. "They are by no means irrelevant to the process. But if you look over the last several decades, you've seen a very sharp decline in the power of the authorizing committees and a very sharp increase in the power of the appropriations committees." It's understandable, he says, that the executive branch might think it is wasting time dealing with authorizing committees and decide "just to focus on the appropriations committee, where the decision is probably going to be made that will really count." He notes the development of a new science—drafting language that is really authorizing language to put into an appropriations bill.

Why is this happening? It shouldn't, according to the House and Senate rules that enforce the separation of the authorization and appropriations processes. Among other transgressions, they forbid the inclusion of legislative language in appropriations bills. Yet to enforce these provisions, it's necessary to raise a point of order—formally invoke the rules. And the rules can also be waived by suspending them.

"If I had a scale of whom you should pay attention to, I would clearly start with the appropriators," is the realistic advice of another onetime member of the House. "If you're going to spend time and effort getting to know people, it's those in the appropriations process. You try to build a leadership program that involves the White House, that is bipartisan, that involves the appropriators, that plays off the authorizers. Usually, lesson number one, the appropriators are going to win. So take that to the bank, regardless of the issue." Or, as a former congressional staffer puts it:

When there's a fight between the appropriators and the authorizers, stick with the appropriators. They get a shot at you every single year.

Don't let this advice unbalance your approach too much, however. The same people who offer it also warn against neglecting the authorizing committees. This is where the day-to-day oversight of what you do resides. Authorizing committees are "your champions," says one, "who have invested a lot in your bureaucracy. Don't ignore them." Make certain you don't "mess around with your authorizing committee," says another, since they "can make your life miserable. Don't work on your appropriators without letting the people you really work with, the subcommittee chairs, the ranking members, know what you're doing and why you're doing it. Don't think the appropriators are where the only action is and you can forget these other guys."

Legislators and Their Constituencies

Another factor not to overlook is the relationship between members of Congress and the people they represent. They are not just those whose votes sent the member to Congress last time around. They are individuals and groups with businesses, economic interests, issues, causes, and special situations the member is expected to look out for. Some of them may not necessarily be confined to the member's home district or state. Together, all these constituencies come first in every member's daily thoughts—not least because they matter decisively in an objective that preoccupies every member: re-election. "People who deal with Congress deal in peril if they don't recognize the incredible interconnection that members of Congress have with their constituents," observes a former member. "It tends to be the way they learn about a lot of what they know. They learn by anecdote, by the individual case of what went wrong in a business, what went wrong for an individual, what went right at the Social Security Administration." A former colleague from the other side of the aisle agrees: "The most significant driving force for any member of the House or Senate is his or her origins—the district or the state."

Recognizing the many differences between House and Senate, smart political appointees will tailor their approaches accordingly. House members are "better prepared," but "more provincial," according to a veteran of service in that chamber. Senators are less prepared, which means their personal and committee staffers swing greater weight. "But senators have a broader view. You may have a quicker, more positive decision on your behalf with a member of the Senate because of the more reflective nature of that body." Depending on where they are in the election cycle, senators also have far more time to deal with the issues. A good rule of thumb is to think of House and Senate as almost separate entities, while never considering one more important than the other.

Relationships

"If you keep the Congress involved, there are no surprises," says an agency head. "They may not always like what you do, but at least they're not surprised. They don't read it in the paper and think, gee, I didn't know anything about that." A senior white House official makes the same point: "They feel worse about reading it in the paper than if you call and tell them that they can't get what they want. No surprises."

If you're trying to develop or strengthen relationships on the Hill, she suggests finding ways for members of the Congress "to share the credit for what you're doing." For example, invite them to events, to tour facilities, to visit programs. If you're having a press conference about something they are concerned with, ask them to join you. In other words, "give them some ownership of the issues, bring them into the process." Be sure in this that you are being bipartisan about it. Don't limit it to just members of your own party. And "look to the members of your committee and then members beyond that. Get them to help you with their expertise."

A lawyer and lobbyist who also served in the Congress recommends being proactive. *Initiate contact with them.* Say *"I'm working on these topics and I know they are of concern to you, your district, your committee, you personally."* Say *you've got scientists or engineers, social workers or nurses or doctors, whatever it is, you have people that can answer some of their questions on those subjects and they should put you down as a resource. Ultimately they need information from you about the topics that you deal with, so why not make it an open-ended offer to begin with? It's much better to offer the help than have somebody serve a Freedom of Information Act subpoena on you.*

You can also make the same offer to staff people who work on given issues for members or committees. Do the same thing with chairs and ranking members of committees. This can have a variety of payoffs. For instance:

It could be in the waning days of one of these omnibus bills that you get a phone call and your input makes the difference in somebody being stuck or willing to bend a little bit. In the final hours of congressional sessions, bending a little bit is what it's all about.

"That doesn't mean you have to co-opt the policy of your department," says this same experienced Hill observer. "It doesn't mean that you have to turn your policy inside out. In a great many instances, it means having information available in which to make a reasoned choice. You have the key to much of the information." If you don't choose to give that key to decision makers in the Congress to use now and then, they may see you as "hiding something or unwilling to help—and that's not good for anybody."

Recently, when a big agency published certain information as required by law, it put some people on the Hill into a serious snit. Here's what happened, related by the head of the agency:

When we first implemented that by the date required, there was a huge uproar about the way we were doing it. Some on the committees were very upset. We went over and said, "Look, we know, we see, we hear, this is not the way it should be, let's work and try to figure out how we can fix this." If we had responded very defensively, and taken sort of an arm's-length approach, I think we would have been in some kind of a war. But that wasn't our point of view. We were not trying to make this thing work badly, we just didn't quite figure it out right. So we said, "Come in and help us." And they did, and we've made it better. So I think the approach is not to be defensive when things go wrong, and to solicit help from all quarters. When you can't accommodate somebody's specific desire, be very up front about why that is. By and large, that has worked pretty well so far.

Oversight

Very few high-level administration appointees in the last 50 years have not felt the thrust (some would call it the sting) of congressional oversight. A less polite term, one you'll encounter frequently, is micromanagement. Oversight means the Congress' responsibility to supervise federal agencies in their program and budget management, their progress toward stated goals, their problems and prospects, and much else. In the process, legislators are supposed to gather information to assist its decisions on designing and paying for government's efforts to run the country's public business. Onerous though it can be, federal agency political managers must learn to work in businesslike fashion with congressional exercise of the oversight function.

The oversight role normally resides in the congressional authorizing committees. It can take the form of committee hearings, field trips, official requests for information, informal inquiries, simple phone calls, and a variety of other mechanisms. Legislators quite naturally use the opportunity for related purposes—to speak for their constituents, promote a point of view, commend or criticize, uphold or undermine. Oversight is a necessary but imperfect function that depends for effectiveness on the willingness of the executive branch and the Congress to work together. Here's how a past House member views it:

There can be too much oversight, without any doubt—too much demand for information and documentation that is not looked at. But a lot of this demand arises from frustration. A member will ask an executive branch official to do this or that. The official says, "yes, that's absolutely right, Congressman, I agree with you wholeheartedly," and walks out the door and nothing ever happens. This gets very frustrating, and members feel the executive branch is not paying any attention, not consulting, not taking them seriously.

The inevitable result?

The only way to get the attention of the executive branch is (something incisive like) dropping in an amendment they don't like. In their view, that's micromanaging, and it probably is. It arises out of a frustration over the lack of serious dialogue between the two branches and the feeling that the executive branch often looks upon the Congress as an obstacle to be overcome, not as a partner in the process. If you have that frame of mind, you're in deep trouble with the Congress.

On the level of personal attitude and behavior on the Hill, a former congressman cautions executive branch managers not to "get personal at any time with arguments or issues." That watchword advice is one of the fundamental truths about the Congress—universally recognized and applicable as much to relationships between members themselves as between members and administration officials:

Remember that today's adversary may be tomorrow's ally.

And some related advice:

Don't be put off by an initial hostile attitude. Sometimes it seems hostile on the surface, but dealing with Congress and the staff is a very personal thing. Call up the staff person of the member that appears hostile and try to have a meeting. You're sure not going to get anywhere if you don't try to have the meeting.

One of the former congressmen quoted earlier takes this further. "Don't grovel," he says. "State your case, but don't be submissive or appear to be weak. Don't be in a situation where members think you're their vassal."

Members are interested in you, just as you are in them, and for the same reason: because you can do something for them. "You're part of a legislative process that's important to them. Don't feel that you're the supplicant in the relationship."

The final word on personal behavior is the old maxim, a cliché but a useful one, quoted by an agency assistant secretary, suggesting that one can "catch more flies with honey than vinegar."

Getting Things Done

Whatever your objective with the Congress, immediate or longer term, achieving it will require a variety of strategies, tactics, or combinations of each. On this question, the best take comes from people who have been the targets of these various approaches while serving in the House and Senate.

One direct approach is lobbying—personal contact with members to enlist their support of a program, a funding request, or other desired action. Depending on what you're seeking, this can be a tough, often frustrating, mission. Yet a former congressman of long service thinks the executive branch puts too few resources into it. "An administration cannot do an effective job if it only trusts three or four people to come to the Hill and lobby, or starts too late," he says. He views the 1999 failure to ratify the comprehensive test ban treaty as a "classic example" of that. "You've got to start early and you've got to stay with it. You have to be flexible according to the members' level of understanding of the issue. You have to consult very broadly, not just with a few." In his experience, the executive branch often makes the "big-time" mistake of confining its lobbying to members of the committee with jurisdiction over the issue.

Naturally, executive branch lobbying has to fight for congressional time and attention with legions of lobbyists for commercial and other nongovernment interest groups ranged along a very long spectrum. These people are specialists in what they do, devote full time to it, and can call on experience, resources, and techniques not available to the executive branch. They are also far better paid. Comparing their objectives on the Hill with those of the executive branch risks distortion or oversimplification; often, it's an apples-and-oranges comparison. But there are times when the interests of both coincide to a point where some form of alliance can be useful.

Among a number of indirect approaches to desired action in the Congress are those endorsed by a cabinet secretary with prior service in the House. "How do you get members' attention? Ask their colleagues to talk to them. That is probably the best way to get their support—a neglected way, but critically important. Next best is editorials in their home state newspapers. Generate those through your public affairs office. That has strong impact. Be careful that it isn't obvious that you're doing it. Third: phone calls rather than written material. Phone calls from live people in interest and stakeholders groups make more of an impact than letters, computer e-mail, telegrams, or faxes."

Also recommended is a continuous process of educating members on your issue or objective. *Go to the power centers outside of your committee, the whips, the Hispanic caucus, black caucus. If it's a children's issue, there are a lot of caucuses that deal with children. Go to members who belong to informal groups that might be responsive to your issue. Be creative, tenacious, and persistent.*

Many agencies have congressional liaison offices, sometimes headed by an official at the assistant secretary level. It's their job to shepherd an agency's legislative requests, track the progress of bills through the committee and floor processes, and maintain the agency's relationships on the Hill. They also assist in preparations for testimony by agency officials, spot opportunities to negotiate deals or compromises and do some hand-holding with individual members—committee chairs, ranking members, others with power or influence over the fate of a given issue. "Generally, they're very good," says this agency head about congressional liaison operations. "On the whole, very competent people." However, he cautions, they tend to get too tight with their key congressional contacts, to develop what in other realms might be called clientitis. "Many of them have good instincts," he says, "but if you have to err when taking their advice, be a little bolder than what they recommended."

Another cabinet secretary and onetime congressman says an appointee's job "is to carry out the policy of the president. Not to do it blindly, but with good judgment." Presidents, he observes, don't need "sycophants who just parrot everything without thinking through what will help get the message and the policy through." What they do need is the use of independent judgment and wisdom in working with the Congress. "Don't be afraid to use those qualities in the process as long as you're not working at cross purposes with what the policy objectives are." From that flows a further point: Assets like integrity, insight, and discretion in an executive branch leader earn trust on the Hill and are likely to carry that individual further.

Dealing with Individual Members

From the wealth of comment and counsel tendered by those who have served in the Congress, some common keynotes emerge when it comes to individual legislators and the do's and don'ts of working with them.

Members today, says one of their colleagues, have several roles. They are legislators, politicians, and educators. They are students who must learn quickly. They are advocates for their constituents and communities, dignitaries invited to every function in their state or district, to say nothing of many events in Washington and abroad. They are traveling fact finders. They are deal makers.

And, we can add, never forget they are fund-raisers, driven to invest disproportionate time in the effort to be re-elected.

To get the most out of your one-on-one contacts with them while side-stepping the pitfalls, the following points can help:

- Understand members' relevance to your concerns. Are they on the committees that you deal with or particularly involved in your issues? When you're planning to call on a member, explore the political framework of what you are seeking. Is the issue you will discuss a plus or a minus for the member? Is it a problem to be on your side or an easy issue to help you with? How well will it play back in their district?

- For you, the most important person in a member's office is not the chief of staff, the legislative assistant, the appropriations person, or the substantive foreign policy expert. It's the scheduler. A former congressman says, "Things got so busy for me in latter years that I had to schedule an appointment with my scheduler in order to see what I was doing."

- When you visit a member, state right away why you're there. Be succinct, professional, and candid about what is in your interest. Don't ramble. Think about what tough questions might be thrown at you. Leave before your welcome runs out.

- Don't try to make the member an expert on the subject. Make short, direct points that zero in so the member understands what you're talking about. The member's staff person on whatever your issue is will be much more informed. You'll want to talk at length with that individual and perhaps provide some briefing materials (which the member won't read). But some members will know more about the issue than you. So be ready to deal with various members at various levels of comprehension.

- Members won't always object if your response to something they want is really a non-response. This is especially true if a member's request is something absurdly unreal like, "My constituent Dolly Jackson was in Paris for three days and wants to be ambassador to France." Members often try to deal with such problems by bucking them to the executive branch. In this case, if you answer that the lady isn't likely to get the job because she doesn't sound qualified for it, you've taken care of that member's problem.

- Don't assume that because members disagree heatedly in public that there is some antipathy between them. Public differences don't necessarily mean private differences as well. Quite often, members of different parties, or those who are adversaries in public, are good friends privately.

- Don't be afraid to say that what the member said about you or your issue was unfair and you want to explain why. Don't appear to be totally submissive, as if you've been whacked and must make amends. Remember that you're all in a political process, and in the executive branch you are dealing with the Congress on a very professional basis. It helps sometimes to put a little edge on what you need to get done.

CHAPTER FIVE

Working with the Media

John H. Trattner
Senior Writer and Editor
Council for Excellence in Government

This essay was originally published as part of "Becoming an Effective Political Executive: 7 Lessons from Experienced Appointees" in January 2001, with a second edition in January 2005.

Working with the Media

(The italicized quotes below are drawn from interviews of presidential appoin-
*tees for **The 2000 Prune Book** by John H. Trattner (Washington, D.C.: Council*
for Excellence in Government and the Brookings Institution Press, 2000) and
from panelists who took part in orientation conferences for new appointees
conducted by The Council and the White House from 1997 to 1999.)

In today's Washington, good news is usually less interesting to media
covering the federal government than bad news. It probably always will
be—for all kinds of reasons, people simply pay more attention to bad news
and, therefore, so do the media. It's just human nature. Bad news concern-
ing your agency doesn't have to be a hanging offense, however. Yet, afraid
of generating bad news, people who run federal agencies sometimes fall into
the trap of trying to make no news at all. And there you have the essence of
the media challenge for federal leaders.

A federal agency with a good media operation has several things going
for it. First, an agency that doesn't wait to be asked—that finds creative
ways to attract objective, positive coverage and tells its story honestly and
factually—can make and keep a favorable impression among people everywhere. That will boost the agency's ability to perform well across the board.
Reporters and editors respect an institution that is accessible and helps them
do their jobs. Implicitly or explicitly, that gets reflected in what they report.
The results are not lost on that agency's citizen customers, congressional
overseers, other government agencies, and the public at large.

Example: When the Defense Department prepared to deploy U.S.
troops to peacekeeping duties in Bosnia in 1996, it knew all too well that
a lot of public opinion in this country opposed the move. Already skeptical about the need for a U.S. peacekeeping role, Americans also worried
about combat casualties in a distant war. To turn the situation around, the
Pentagon adopted an assertive, consistent communications strategy on Bosnia that portrayed the troop deployment as a mission to help others help
themselves, not to take sides or dictate terms. As part of their assignment,
American troops got media training to help them convey that message.
Given easy access to American soldiers in Bosnia, journalists reported to
American audiences on their life and work there. About a month into the
mission, a major opinion poll showed that more than half the American
public supported U.S. policy in Bosnia. Later, the American military pres-
ence was stretched beyond its original one year—and U.S. troops remain
there today. Almost no one has argued, then or since, that they should come
home. It was a classic example of how to take your case to the public via
the media and win.

Handling Bad News

Second, since bad news is inevitable in the life of any institution, an agency that knows what to do at such times can minimize the impact.

Bad news is not like wine or cheese—it does not improve with age. You have a choice. Do you want to have a one-day story that says you screwed up? Or a three- or four-day story that says you screwed up and lied about how you screwed up and you tried to make it go away and it didn't go away? Better to just get it over with.

"The other day," a television correspondent notes, "the FBI announced the arrest of a veteran employee of the Drug Enforcement Administration (DEA), an auditor who had been skimming thousands of dollars for years from the DEA. The DEA put out a press release saying, here's who the person is, here's what the FBI said he did, here's what we've done to try to fix it. Boom—the story just absolutely vanished like paint thinner. Because they stepped up to the plate and said the guy's a bum and he's out. That's exactly the right way to handle it."

Or take the story of the costly Mars Polar Lander mission in late 1999. It failed when, despite repeated attempts, no contact was ever established with the spacecraft after it was to touch down. National Aeronautics and Space Administration (NASA) was on the front pages for days, with much of the coverage unfavorable. But the agency kept putting out whatever news and comment it could about the mission. "Every time we learn something about what's happening on Mars or isn't happening, we have told the media as we learn it," a NASA official told a network anchorman at the time. But he wondered whether it was worth it, "since it seems to me we're just going to continue to get the bad news over and over again." He wanted to know how the anchorman saw the situation. "I think NASA took a very candid approach," was the reply. "You handled it the way it should have been handled." Maybe there was no way to put a good face on the story, the anchorman said, "but every step along the way, the audience and I were being informed of what was going on. I think NASA is to be congratulated." He went on to say:

We all have our share of bad news, personal, professional, agency. You get the story out there—in my view, you're going to be a lot better off trying to cut your losses early and getting your case out than you are in delay, delay, delay.

There is a third point here. The assets an agency builds in its proactive mode are often just as useful when it must adopt a reactive stance. A federal agency official tells a story that broke about tainted milk when she was an advisor to a state governor. The milk had been contaminated by bad dairy feed. Reporters were demanding to know immediately when the state was going to pull all milk.

We just invited a group of them in to talk. We told them it was easy to think the big issue was when were we going to pull the milk. But you also had to think through a lot of other things. If you pulled all the milk, what were you going to do with it? You can't just go pour it out, because it seeps into ground water. And what about the years spent getting people to drink milk because of the things in it that are good for them? We said, let's talk through this domino effect and the fact that a lot of careful thinking has to be done. And the reason we were able to say those things, at a time when the national press was really pouring in, was because we had offered proactive briefings, trying to make sure there would be a real dialogue going on when something's happening. They were people that we had built good relationships with. I know that's what helped us through that.

Offense or Defense?

"There are generally two kinds of agencies," says the network television anchorman. "One has an agency head or press chief who, when the press calls, says 'let's see what we can do.' The other is the 'oh, my God, it's the media, now what?' kind. Chances are the first kind of agency is going to get a lot better treatment, because there's going to be more cooperation there. I think it takes a sea change in mentality."

No question—spending less time in a reactive crouch and more on advance planning, effective public communications, and outreach is the best investment for working with the media. We've already seen the value of proactivity. What are the other specific elements of that strategy?

Communicators. A former agency public affairs official who was also a television reporter and anchor says, "Get your communication people in on things early, not when decisions and actions are fully formed." Indeed, government public affairs people have long argued that they should be on hand when policy is taking shape, not after the fact. That allows them to understand what the policy is to be and ask all the tough questions now that the press will ask later. It permits them to see to the vital, often neglected, task of coordinating an agency's public communication with other relevant government institutions. Sometimes their participation can help improve the policy decision itself. Sometimes it will alter the way policy is to be presented publicly. Listen to the advice of a leading national public opinion expert:

In government, you need to spend a lot more time figuring out this is going to be the story, this is how we're going to do it, this is how we're going to use the secretary or the under secretary, this is the position.

So one fundamental of good media strategy is that communications people have to be there on offense and defense. It is promotion and damage control, all wrapped into one. Years ago, a government communicator put this concept into words for all time: Public affairs people want to be there "at the take-offs as well as the landings" (when it will also be their job to pick up the pieces if things don't go well).

This is not a question of policy wonks versus communication people. The question is: What's the mission? If you're going to put together a good program, you've got to think of what all the down sides are. Somebody has to be at the table seeing it from that other perspective.

Technique. Next, agency seniors who deal personally with journalists on an individual basis should have one or two rules of thumb in mind. "Go in with an agenda," says a White House official. "That takes some skill so that you don't simply ignore the question on the table. You need to answer the question asked. But, as quickly as you can in the construct of that question, get to what it is that you want to say." Don't give a journalist total control of the agenda. "If you have something to say, make sure you say it. Don't have to offer the excuse later that, 'Well, she never really asked me about X.'"

An agency assistant secretary who meets fairly often with reporters says he usually starts by speaking on a background basis for a while (meaning that what he says cannot be attributed to him by name or position). That's "just to get a feel for what the reporter is about and what the questions are." He thinks it's important to "get a sense of what role you're being cast in for the interview. You have to figure out where the reporter's coming from, what kind of a story is being written, and then you can decide how you can write your own part. If they're just casting you as the dumb government bureaucrat, chances are you want to avoid saying anything that will confirm the impression." Other specific advice:

- Respond promptly to calls from journalists, giving yourself the chance to add the administration's or your own personal point of view to the story and supply information that expands its scope or meaning.
- When possible, especially on policy issues, work both sides of a newspaper—the editorial board as well as the reporters. "Sometimes an editorial board takes wrong-headed or uninformed positions," a correspondent observes frankly. "They do their thing and they don't usually share it with the reporting staff."
- Use the specialized media, the "trade press," in addition to the mainline media. These publications and television channels can make a big difference on particular issues on which they focus. As one reporter joked, "I'm sure, if you work in the Department of Housing and Urban Development, there's a *Modern Bricks Magazine*. Or *Food Stamp Monthly* if you're at Agriculture."

Quality. The third element of a media operation that works is the quality of what's being said. Journalists are often in a hurry, driven by deadlines and competition. Government leaders don't face those particular kinds of pressures. They have less excuse for being inaccurate in what they convey publicly.

The news cycle today is constant. It's not just the evening paper and the evening news. There is talk radio and the net and the cable channels. So there is terrible tension between getting the story right and getting it right away. You need to do both, but it's more important to get it right. The press puts a higher priority on getting it right away. Their biggest fear is they will be in a lot more trouble for being late than for being wrong. You have to have a higher priority on getting it right. You've got to have your credibility. It's the most important thing, it's why you were brought into this government, in part, and it's what you need to take out of this government with you when you leave.

Never lie in speaking with journalists in any official capacity. Sooner or later, but inevitably, you'll be caught and your credibility—assuming there's any left—will never be the same. It's also bad for the people you work with, your agency, and your administration. Be as factual and accurate as possible.

But also remember the story about the witness being sworn in at court who, when asked to tell the truth, the whole truth, and nothing but the truth, asked, "Which one do you prefer, judge?" In other words, you don't have to volunteer information that isn't being asked for, but what you do say should be the truth.

Make sure people can understand what you are saying. If a government communication is unintelligible, a university media expert argues, people assume the agency or office that put it out is trying to hide something. Here's a perfect example, offered by the television reporter cited earlier:

The deputy assistant secretary is there, in all of his deputy assistant secretary-hood, trying to explain this and he's not speaking English. He's saying that "the share of the youth cohort that has sustainable exposure to illicit substances has been trending downward," when what he really means is fewer kids are using drugs. So speak English. Ask yourself if your next-door neighbor will understand what you're saying. How would you say it on the telephone to your mother? Write it down that way.

Don't let a crisis or emergency situation, destroy the quality of what you say publicly or affect how you handle the media. "Take a breath and tell them you have to get back to them," says the former senior White House executive—"you have to track it down, round it up, find out." Don't jump out with statements or position papers before you know what's actually happening. "It's just a question of experience and judgment," as the White House official sees it. "Sometimes, if you just let it go, it turns out not as big a crisis as you thought it might be."

Capable press spokespersons are vital. Maybe they have been journalists themselves, maybe not, but they have to be people who can talk with calm confidence to the press in any setting, on any basis, individually or in formal briefings. Good spokespersons are articulate, informed, and up-to-date on the institutions they represent, their policies, and their actions. Remember that spokespersons are only as good as the quality of their information and access to policy makers. Deny them either of these, and you cripple their ability to advance or defend the interests of their agencies or the administration. Make them mouthpieces only, without reasonable latitude to think, inquire, or speak on their own, and the media will ignore them. Take them into your confidence and trust, and they will help you get the results you're looking for.

Surviving in the government/media culture. The fourth important component in a good media strategy is productive working relationships with journalists, in which each side has reasonable confidence and can expect reasonable treatment. Right, you might well say—and, in the current Washington climate, about as likely as the sun rising in the west.

True, government and media co-exist in a wary relationship too often characterized by mutual suspicion. True, there are certain mind-sets on both sides—among them, that government executives are obfuscating, over-loyal, condescending, usually ready to run for protective cover; that reporters are imperious, self-important, poorly informed, vulnerable to the instincts of the herd. No one would deny that there is more than a little justification for these sentiments. But they shouldn't dominate the scene. Consider the following excerpts from the comments of three of the print and television journalists quoted earlier as they focused on this question of attitude:

Newspaper correspondent: *"Reporters don't expect you to make yourself look bad or your agency look bad. In fact, a lot of times, part of our mission is to present a balanced story, whatever it is. To be fair, we try to let each side make its very best argument. We'll sort through a lot of listening to try to get the kernel of what your case is. Don't presume that someone is coming at you with any particular agenda or ideological bias or even to make you look bad."*

Television anchor: *"Credibility is all we have. Without it we have no reason to do what we do. Why should we risk our credibility by misrepresenting the information that is given us? We may test the information. But it would be foolhardy of us, whose livelihood depends on credibility, to try to manipulate the facts until they become non-facts."*

Newspaper correspondent: *"I expect people to tell me the truth and deal with me in good faith and they only get one chance. If they don't, then I know where they are and can never trust them again. That doesn't mean I would never talk to them again. It's just that I have a sense of what their ethics are."*

Television correspondent: *"Ninety percent of people in government think the media only care when they screw up. Wrong. Yes, the media are fascinated when government screws up. Bad news is interesting. But the media love it when people in government win, when they succeed. Help them help you tell your own story."*

Newspaper correspondent: *"It's a really delicate human relationship. In the end we're just all people and we don't want to burn our sources. We want to be able to come back to you on another day and have you take our phone calls and give us information. But we don't want to be in the bag for somebody either. It's a delicate line to walk."*

Leaks

At some point most political leaders, appointed as well as elected, find themselves dealing with the consequences of anonymously disclosed information, or leaks. Typically, a leak is the product of a one-on-one contact with a journalist initiated by an individual with the intention of exerting a specific effect. Because of its total lack of sourcing, any information that gets into the media in this way needs extra scrutiny.

How do you know a leak when you see one? While it's not always simple, one frequent clue is the complete anonymity of the source—though that by itself is not conclusive. Second, since they are agenda-driven, leaked stories usually have some kind of target: a policy, a cause, an action, an individual. Third, now and then a story based on a leak will claim to reveal confidential or surprising information, previously undivulged, perhaps with a whiff of the sensational.

Bottom Line

The evidence suggests that an objective, outgoing stance with the media over the long term is likely to produce similar treatment in return. Will there be exceptions and aberrations? Of course. Can a federal department or agency afford to relax when its relations with the media are in good shape? Of course not. It should carefully think out its media operation and carefully manage it—all the time. There's no such thing as a free ride with the media. Whatever the degree of pain or pleasure you think you are deriving from media coverage of your agency, the coverage isn't going to go away. It only makes sense, therefore, to invest the extra effort that makes it as positive and beneficial as possible.

PART III

Working with
Your Organization

CHAPTER SIX

Working to Transform
Your Organization

Mark A. Abramson
Executive Director
IBM Center for The Business of Government

Paul R. Lawrence
Partner, IBM Business Consulting Services
and
Partner-in-Charge
IBM Center for The Business of Government

This essay was published in "Becoming an Effective Political Executive: 7 Lessons from Experienced Appointees" in January 2001, with a second edition in January 2005, and also appears in Transforming Organizations, *Mark Abramson and Paul Lawrence, eds. (Rowman & Littlefield, 2001).*

Working to Transform Your Organization

Transforming organizations is hard work. It is not for the fainthearted or thin-skinned. A leader is not going to win many new friends or popularity contests by undertaking major transformation initiatives. In spite of the difficulty, we expect transformation to continue as 20th century bureaucracies are streamlined into high-performing 21st century organizations. For executives at the helm of these changes, there is much to learn from the experience of others.

The key question is: How do leaders successfully transform organizations? To better understand the transformation challenge, the IBM Center for The Business Government supported a series of case studies of the most successful transformation initiatives of the 1990s in the federal government. The goal was to document these initiatives and identify lessons learned that could be shared with other executives seeking to change their organization. Organizations selected for case studies were:

- Department of Defense (DoD) under Deputy Secretary (and then Secretary) William Perry. The DoD case study focuses on procurement reform within the Department of Defense, including key roles played by Under Secretary of Defense for Acquisition and Technology Paul Kaminski, Deputy Under Secretary for Acquisition Reform Colleen Preston, and Administrator of the Office of Federal Procurement Policy Steve Kelman
- Federal Emergency Management Agency (FEMA) under Director James Lee Witt
- National Aeronautics and Space Administration (NASA) under Administrator Daniel S. Goldin
- Veterans Health Administration (VHA), Department of Veterans Affairs, under Under Secretary for Health Dr. Kenneth Kizer

From these case studies of the four organizations, eight common lessons emerged about how leaders successfully undertake large-scale transformation initiatives.

Lesson 1: Select the Right Person

The four transformation initiatives all began with the appointment of the right person to the right job in the right organization at the right time. Steven Daniels and Carolyn L. Clark-Daniels write, "Recruitment … may be one of the president's … most critical decisions at the start of an administration" (Daniels and Clark-Daniels, 2000). In selecting James Lee Witt to head FEMA, President Clinton selected an individual with extensive experience in emergency management, a sharp departure from past appointments to the

Lessons Learned about Transforming Organizations

Lesson 1: Select the right person

Lesson 2: Clarify the mission

Lesson 3: Get the structure right

Lesson 4: Seize the moment

Lesson 5: Communicate, communicate, and communicate

Lesson 6: Involve key players

Lesson 7: Engage employees

Lesson 8: Persevere

agency. Director Witt then used his influence in the appointment process to select a team of political executives who were all experienced and highly qualified in emergency management. Daniels and Clark-Daniels conclude that the cumulative experience of the senior political appointees vastly improved the organization's capability and made its transformation possible.

The selection of highly qualified, experienced individuals was also key to the success of transformation at DoD. Kimberly A. Harokopus writes: "The leaders of defense procurement reform were remarkably well suited for the tough job at hand. They all had experience with the acquisition process—some as practitioners, others as researchers, still others as members of the defense industry seeking to comply with the sometimes byzantine set of procurement rules. With the exception of Kelman, each had previously worked inside the Pentagon as a military or civilian leader. Each had recognized the failings of the defense acquisition system and each had struggled to remedy it—through advisory boards, informal correspondence to defense leaders, and published scholarly works. It was as if they had been preparing for years to meet this challenge" (Harokopus, 2000).

From his analysis of the VHA transformation, Gary J. Young writes, "VHA's transformation highlights the importance of having leaders whose backgrounds and experiences fit the needs of the transformation" (Young, 2000). Young dates the start of the VHA transformation initiative with the appointment of Dr. Ken Kizer. Young concludes that Dr. Kizer proved to be a highly effective leader for the VHA transformation. His effectiveness, writes Young, was largely the result of the match between his professional experience and the needs of the transformation. " ... [A]lthough Dr. Kizer was new to VHA, he did have substantial leadership experience in the public sector.... Dr. Kizer was an astute student of innovations in the financing and delivery of health care services. He had witnessed many innovations first-hand through his professional experiences in California...."

The appointment of Dan Goldin at NASA also demonstrates the importance of making the right match to the right job. W. Henry Lambright writes: "The choice of Dan Goldin was fortuitous given the need. He was a good match for the organization and times. He replaced a man who was forced to leave because he was not viewed as the right person for the challenges facing the agency.... On the whole, ... his original appointment and retention by Clinton were good for NASA and the country" (Lambright, 2001).

Lesson 2: Clarify the Mission

Witt, Dr. Kizer, and Goldin followed similar paths during the early days of their tenure. James Lee Witt spent his initial days refocusing FEMA's mission on emergency management rather than national preparedness. This change in focus redefined the agency's primary client to be disaster victims and served as the central tenet of all the management reforms that followed.

At VHA, Dr. Ken Kizer spent his early days spearheading the creation of a vision for the transformation of the organization. In describing the blueprint report, *Vision for Change,* Young writes, "The document articulated the basic philosophy, principles, and organizational framework to which a transformed VHA would adhere."

At NASA, Dan Goldin went through a similar process. Lambright writes, "Given the budget constraint Goldin faced when he first was appointed, he was forced to deal with the question, 'What do I do to bring NASA's expectations into line with likely funding?' His answer was not to eliminate programs. Rather, he intended to promote technological and managerial reforms that would allow the agency to carry out all of its existing programs and even provide funds to make new starts."

Lesson 3: Get the Structure Right

While leaders frequently shy away from structural reorganizations because of the difficulty in doing so, Dr. Kizer, Witt, and Goldin all decided reorganizations were crucial to their ability to transform their organization. Within the first year of the transformation, Dr. Kizer proposed and enacted a sweeping change in the agency's organizational structure. The new structure entailed the reorganization of all VHA operating units into 22 networks. Marilyn A. DeLuca concludes that large-scale change frequently necessitates organizational redesign. DeLuca writes: "The agency's structure should facilitate reform, and consideration should be given to the function, size, and organizational placement of various managerial and advisory units within the organization. The distance between the agency 'center' and 'field' is important to ensure sound communication and exchange of information. As too much change can create chaos, thoughtfully planned and executed redesign is key. Such redesign should consider the reform objectives as well as organizational culture and the existing productive linkages" (DeLuca, 2000).

To better structure the agency to pursue its newly refocused mission on disaster management, FEMA created new agency directorates organized around the basic functions of emergency management. Director Witt separated the operational components of the State and Local Programs and Support Directorate into separate Preparedness, Mitigation, and Response and Recovery Directorates. In a finding similar to that of DeLuca, Daniels and Clark-Daniels describe the reorganization process: "Most public officials recognize the importance of matching agency structure to agency policy goals. Implementing a program using existing agency structures and procedures invites policy conflict and the inefficient use of personnel and resources. One of the leading causes of the proliferation of government agencies is the recognition that matching agency structure to agency mission is easier in a new agency than an ongoing one."

Like Dr. Kizer and Witt, Goldin also concluded that organizational realignment was necessary. Six months after his arrival, Goldin reorganized the Office of Space Science and Applications (OSSA). In reorganizing OSSA, Lambright writes, Goldin wanted more visibility for the earth observation and life science elements of the enterprise. By splitting OSSA into three offices, earth observations and life sciences would each have its own director.

Lesson 4: Seize the Moment

The key to the success of any executive is finding precisely the right time in the organization's history to undertake large-scale transformation. The DoD team, Dr. Kizer, and Goldin all used the changing external environment to bring about internal transformation of their organizations. Regarding the DoD team, Harokopus writes, "The era of defense procurement reform was also an era of political, technological, and national security changes…. While these conditions created a climate for reform, it was key individuals, taking advantage of those circumstances, which made the crucial difference. Opportunity is worthless unless it is seized. These leaders recognized the opportunity for tremendous change in public management and they acted on it."

The situation at the Veterans Health Administration was similar. By the early 1990s, Young reports that VHA had become out of sync with the prevailing trends in the delivery of health services. The advent of health maintenance organizations and developments in medical technology had begun the shift away from inpatient-based medicine to outpatient-based primary care medicine. Dr. Kizer himself concluded that change within VHA must move in harmony with environmental or externally focused change. Dr. Kizer writes, "Top managers, particularly those in the public sector, cannot hope to stand against the 'forces of nature'.... In the case of the VHA, that means being in sync with broad trends, such as the national revolution in health care, the explosion of biomedical research and knowledge, the shift to 'an information society,' and the aging of the eligible VHA population."

In examining reform within both the United States Veterans Health Administration and the United Kingdom's National Health Service, DeLuca observed the importance of finding a "window of opportunity." She concludes that environmental factors, including socioeconomic and political conditions and pressure from the public or interest groups, can often prompt the need for organizational change.

When he was appointed in 1992, Goldin was given the task "to reinvent NASA in the post–Cold War era and take it into the 21st century." Lambright writes, "When Goldin became administrator, many observers saw NASA as a bloated bureaucracy pursuing missions that took too long, cost too much, and used technology that was old by the time it was put into space." In addition, the changing environment also included new foreign policy objectives. The new NASA administrator, reports Lambright, "would have to deal with the foreign policy need of the United States to forge a new relationship with the Russians and the world. Goldin, through the Space Station, made NASA a positive instrument of this policy need, elevating NASA to a component of presidential foreign policy and making it more relevant to the times."

All the leaders profiled used real and perceived crises to support and speed up their transformation initiatives. Lambright writes, "A crisis situation creates an organizational need for leadership and willingness of the organization to go along, at least for a while. Goldin proved an effective crisis manager. He seized command of Space Station decision making from those formally in charge and created what was, in effect, a parallel unit under his direction, which redesigned the Space Station."

James Lee Witt effectively used the historically poor reputation of FEMA in 1993 to stimulate change within his organization. The DoD procurement reform team successfully capitalized on the procurement "scandals" of the 1980s to successfully implement procurement changes in the 1990s.

The importance of a perceived crisis cannot be underestimated. Lambright writes: "The lesson is that a crisis can help the leader in forwarding major change. Crisis allows the leader to pull power to himself. Because he spans the boundary across organizational programs and negotiates the space between organization and environment, he is in a strategic position to seize the initiative. He can use a crisis to go beyond incremental to radical change. A leader who successfully leads his organization through a crisis can secure his position, neutralize rivals, and enlarge the change coalition within the organization through his appointees and insiders, who become believers."

Lesson 5: Communicate, Communicate, and Communicate

All the case studies conclude that effective communication is crucial to the success of any transformation initiative. In the case of procurement reform, Harokopus writes: "... each leader sustained a remarkable communications strategy with constant but varied platforms for publicizing their message. From public speeches at symposia, conferences, and industrial gatherings, to brown bag lunches, town-hall-style meetings, and electronic chat sessions, there was always a variety of styles, media, and audience. The end result was an environment charged with enthusiasm over the new possibilities for acquisition."

At FEMA, James Lee Witt concluded that external communication was crucial to reshaping the agency. Daniels and Clark-Daniels report that when Witt arrived, he found that "FEMA was used to operating in anonymity, and had no effective plan for involving the media and, by extension, the public in FEMA operations." Under Witt, the agency reshaped FEMA's communications to actively engage the media throughout the response and recovery period. "By making the agency more accessible and by providing the media with prompt answers and information, FEMA disarmed much of the inevitable criticism that arose in the immediate aftermath of a disaster. More significantly, the agency opened a two-way channel for information between itself and the disaster victims it was serving," write Daniels and Clark-Daniels.

DeLuca also found the importance of communication in her cross-national study of healthcare reform. DeLuca concludes, "Transformation of large systems is best accomplished by setting goals and communicating those objectives both within the organization and to interest groups." Both DeLuca and Young give the Veterans Health Administration a mixed report on communicating to those both inside and outside of VHA. DeLuca writes, "While the goals were clearly communicated to the VISN (Veterans Integrated Service Networks) and medical center executives, communication varied across other levels of staff and was often lacking to interest groups."

Young concludes that failure to effectively communicate was a major weakness of the VHA transformation initiative. Young writes: "VHA's transformation offers another of many examples where conventional communication strategies did not work to keep frontline employees informed during a large-scale change effort. To inform employees about the transformation, the senior leadership team distributed written notices and videotapes, held town meetings, and conducted video conferences. However, the survey data collected as part of this study indicate that these methods of communication were not reaching frontline employees."

Communication was sometimes a problem at NASA under Dan Goldin. Lambright concludes that a hard-driving administrator with a confrontational style can sometimes shut off the flow of communication. "Communication, communication, and more communication in an organization is the answer to heading off disaster. The communication has to flow freely and candidly from the bottom to the top and vice versa. A leader has to work overtime to assure he gets such communication and feedback. This is especially the case where the change process is so strongly pushed from the top. If a leader is perceived as closed-minded by his officials and staff, he will be a barrier to his own reforms," writes Lambright.

Lesson 6: Involve Key Players

In all the case studies, a key to the organization's successful transformation was the realization that there were nongovernmental entities deeply interested and involved in the organization's business. The challenge was then to find innovative ways in which to engage them in support of the organization's mission. In the case of FEMA, Director Witt consistently emphasized the importance of partnerships with state and local governments, nonprofit organizations, and the private sector.

At the Department of Defense, Secretary William Perry clearly recognized the importance of involving the defense contractor industry in the dialogue over procurement reform. Harokopus writes, "Perry's team was convinced that the acquisition community should be the primary source for reform initiatives." Perry, reports Harokopus, made the entire acquisition community—both those inside and outside of government—party to the problem as well as part of the solution. The Department's Process Action Teams (PATs) were charged to seek defense industry involvement in the development of all procurement reforms.

Based on both the experience of the National Health Service and the Veterans Health Administration, DeLuca concludes that it is essential to involve interest groups and pertinent community members in reform discussions and debates around workable strategies. "While interest-group participation may be perceived as slowing the change process or, more commonly, be restricted due to concern that these groups may derail or undermine change, exclusion of interest groups limits the effectiveness of the reforms in the long run. Cooperative partnerships that permit participation in change, an emphasis on communication, and avoidance of perverse incentives minimize dissatisfaction and tension among staff as well as inter-est groups," writes DeLuca.

Lesson 7: Engage Employees

While undertaking organizational transformation, agency leadership must pay special attention to employees. Young reports that while VHA had planned several educational and training initiatives as part of their transformation, most of the initiatives were not in place at the time the agency was undergoing its sweeping change in structure. Looking back, Young concludes that "VHA's senior leadership placed too little emphasis on training and education." As a consequence, Young recommends, "… in situations where swift change is deemed necessary, senior managers should not overlook the importance of training and education to support employees in developing needed skills in a timely manner."

DeLuca also emphasizes the need for staff engagement. She writes, "The manner in which reform is introduced, particularly regarding staff involve-ment and communication, affects the response of staff to the reform process. Leaders should be knowledgeable and sensitive to the process of change, as well as the desired objectives. Employees who are more empowered and engaged in the change are more involved in the reform process."

At the Department of Defense, recognition, awards, and training were integral to the defense reform initiative. Harokopus writes, "Defense pro-curement could not change without acceptance by the practitioners…. The leadership understood that for practitioners to become reform enthusiasts, they would need incentives for accepting change and reinforcement from top leaders. Acquisition practitioners needed to know that their opinions were valued and their participation was essential. As a result, the leaders focused on a strategy that included recognition, awards, and training."

But not all efforts to engage employees succeed. At NASA, Goldin's efforts to encourage a bottom-up strategy were not totally successful. Lambright reports that Goldin "wanted the organization to reach a consen-sus and then interact with the public in creating an even larger consensus for change. Unfortunately, this participative strategy was coupled with financial costs. He ordered 'red and blue' teams to counter one another in downsiz-ing various programs, even as they sought a vision statement and engaged in strategy planning. Cutback planning was a threat to many inside officials."

Lesson 8: Persevere

The final lesson is that it isn't going to be easy. The challenge is described well by Gary Young: "All transformations generate controversy and criticism. Such criticism and controversy often distract leaders of transformations from focusing on the central goals of the change effort. In the case of VHA, the senior leadership kept its sights fixed on key transformation goals while making mid-course correction to address technical problems as they were recognized."

"No transformation will be perfect," writes Young, "and those who oppose the changes will seek to exploit flaws or limitations to derail the effort. Leaders of transformation need to be responsive to legitimate criticisms, but they also must avoid being swallowed up in technical details."

Transforming and revitalizing government organizations is difficult, time-consuming, but is possible. The leaders profiled in these case studies demonstrate that transformation can be done. Executives in both the public and private sector can learn much from the experiences of these leaders.

Bibliography

Daniels, R. Steven, and Carolyn L. Clark-Daniels. "Transforming Government: The Renewal and Revitalization of the Federal Emergency Management Agency." Washington, D.C.: IBM Center for The Business of Government, April 2000.

DeLuca, Marilyn A. "Trans-Atlantic Experiences in Health Reform: The United Kingdom's National Health Service and the United States Veterans Health Administration." Washington, D.C.: IBM Center for The Business of Government, May 2000.

Harokopus, Kimberly A. "Transforming Government: Creating the New Defense Procurement System." Washington, D.C.: IBM Center for The Business of Government, April 2000.

Lambright, W. Henry. "Transforming Government: Dan Goldin and the Remaking of NASA." Washington, D.C.: IBM Center for The Business of Government, March 2001.

Young, Gary J. "Transforming Government: The Revitalization of the Veterans Health Administration." Washington, D.C.: IBM Center for The Business of Government, June 2000.

Note: All five case studies appear in *Transforming Organizations*, edited by Mark A. Abramson and Paul R. Lawrence (Rowman & Littlefield, 2001).

CHAPTER SEVEN

Working with Career Executives to Manage for Results

Dana Michael Harsell
Assistant Professor of Political Science
Hartwick College

This essay was originally published in "Becoming an Effective Political Executive: 7 Lessons from Experienced Appointees," 2nd ed., January 2005.

Working with Career Executives
to Manage for Results

Historically, the relationships between political appointees and career executives have been marked with some degree of tension, especially during a transition in leadership. Career executives are perceived by new appointees as continuing the agenda of the previous political leaders, and new political leaders are perceived by careerists as bringing in a new but unclear agenda of changes that may not be anchored in the context of what the agency does.

However, recent management reforms based in both legislation and presidential direction have created a new environment in many agencies that promotes a joint political/career focus on better managing for results related to agency missions.

Based on in-depth observations in three agencies—the Department of Housing and Urban Development (HUD), the National Aeronautics and Space Administration (NASA), and the Occupational Safety and Health Administration (OSHA) in the Department of Labor—this new environment seems to have contributed to constructive improvements in the relationships between political appointees and career senior executives. The two management reforms that were cited as contributing to this refocused relationship are the Government Performance and Results Act and the President's Management Agenda.

The Government Performance and Results Act. The Government Performance and Results Act of 1993 (GPRA) represents one of the most sweeping managerial reform efforts in the post–World War II period. At its core, it attempts to improve internal agency management by requiring a clear articulation of strategic plans, annual operating plans, and an annual report on performance against the plan for the prior year. GPRA differs from previous reform efforts because it is grounded in statute. As a result, it has successfully survived a transition between two ideologically diverse presidential administrations.

One of the anticipated byproducts of GPRA-mandated changes is that the law seems to be serving as a positive bridge in communications between career managers and political appointees. Data from the three case study agencies demonstrate that GPRA requirements have had a positive effect on the career/political appointee relationships, which traditionally are strained during a transition between political leaders, either between or within the same administration.

These positive, if unanticipated, effects stem from a number of cultural and institutional changes embedded in GPRA's statutory requirements. For example, the law creates a "common language" between these two executive-branch actors, allowing them to engage each other in ways they had not before. This new pattern of engagement was most apparent during the initial transition in political leadership, a time that is often stressful for careerists and political appointees. During the transition, many politicals and careerists engaged each other in a process of formal goal setting and revision, as required by GPRA. The career interviewees in the three agency case studies generally characterized this as greatly exceeding the benefits of the traditional transition dialogues that had taken place in the past. The interviews also suggest that the GPRA process has contributed to a number of more substantively meaningful mutual outputs, and may also inhibit the tendency for political and career leadership to inhabit their separate policy spheres without really interacting with one another.

Since GPRA is grounded in law, agencies are legally accountable for its provisions. GPRA implementation and compliance enjoyed sustained support from both the Clinton administration and a few very vocal "GPRA champions" within Congress. These attributes further set GPRA apart from the litany of administratively based reform efforts that frequently ended with the presidential administrations that inaugurated them.

GPRA also departs from many previous administratively centered reforms as it represents an attempt to rationalize the decision making process through requiring the use and continual development of a number of managerial tools, including mission statements, short-term and long-term strategic plans, performance measurement systems, and the dissemination of agency results to Congress, the Executive and agency stakeholders. While it is impractical to think that any reform can unequivocally rationalize the political process, the evidence from the three case studies suggests that this rationalization process has helped to engage these two sets of actors, promoted deliberation and meaningful interactions, and even encouraged creative tensions between the two.

The President's Management Agenda. The results of the case studies also suggest that GPRA's contributions toward improving communications between career and political executives have been sustained by the most recent executive-based reform effort, the George W. Bush administration's President's Management Agenda (PMA). The PMA is a broad-based executive managerial reform effort that is managed by the Office of Management and Budget (OMB). According to John Kamensky, Senior Fellow at the IBM Center for The Business of Government, the PMA is a strong, disciplined focus on meeting tough but achievable goals. The PMA was designed, in part, to build on the framework established by GPRA.

The PMA seeks to improve agency performance among five government-wide management areas: human capital, competitive sourcing, improved financial management, expanded electronic government, and budget and performance integration. Agency performance is graded on a red/yellow/green scale via OMB's executive branch management scorecard list. The scorecard ranks the performance of 26 executive agencies (14 cabinet departments and 12 independent agencies) along the five management areas. Agencies are given a red, yellow, or green score for each of these criteria on a semi-annual basis; a red score indicates poor performance, yellow indicates mixed results, and green indicates the agency has met or exceeded the standards for success. OMB also developed the Program Assessment Rating Tool (PART) to support the budget and performance integration component of the President's Management Agenda. PART was created on the assumption that GPRA and the PMA share the common goal of linking performance information to the budgetary process, but also on the assumption that much of the performance data generated from GPRA is not being used to inform agency or program decisions.

Analysis of the Three Case Studies

While the GPRA and PMA reform efforts differ somewhat in their orientation (one interviewee described GPRA as a long-term capacity-building exercise and the PMA as a mechanism to achieve shorter-term political goals), they reinforce each other in many substantive ways. The PMA has done much to sustain GPRA in the wake of waning congressional interest, and GPRA serves as an underlying framework to achieve PMA goals. This research also suggests that the GPRA process—and subsequent efforts by the PMA—have laid down and reinforced a managerial framework that has demonstrably enhanced political appointee and career manager relationships by promoting cooperation and helping these two actors overcome natural barriers to consensual management.

Both political and career executives have employed GPRA's statutory results-oriented framework and the executive-centered efforts of the PMA to smooth the often stressful process of transition and to enhance the appointee/careerist relationship more generally. Put simply, the focus of GPRA and the PMA on improved government performance depends in vital ways on reduced tensions between the two basic constituencies of the U.S. executive branch. And structural barriers have, it appears, begun to fall, thanks in part to these reforms.

Given the mandate of GPRA and the PMA to enhance government performance, their effect on this fundamental bureaucratic relationship is vital. Whether these performance management systems can help promote comity and productive relationships is worth exploring in greater depth. Additionally, this research can provide a guide for federal managers to use the management tools established by GPRA and the PMA, especially during future transitions of political leadership when these two executive-branch actors are in the very early stages of forging new working relationships.

Methodology Used to Develop Study Findings

To what extent can existing reform efforts create a bridge between political and career executives? To answer this question, this inquiry assesses the effects of GPRA and the PMA on the career/political appointee relationships using a variety of approaches. Primary data comes from 43 in-depth interviews, the bulk of which were conducted with career managers and political appointees in three case study agencies:

- Department of Housing and Urban Development (HUD)

- National Aeronautics and Space Administration (NASA)

- Occupational Safety and Health Administration (OSHA) in the Department of Labor

Additional interviewees included congressional staffers, personnel from the Office of Management and Budget and the Government Accountability Office, as well as performance management, GPRA, and PMA scholars and practitioners. Other data sources include congressional legislative history, various scholarly assessments of GPRA and the PMA, and specifically GPRA- and PMA-related documents intended for both public and internal consumption.

Agencies have used GPRA to improve both the leadership transition process and subsequent exchanges between political appointees and career executives. Regarding the former, the strategic planning process has brought these two layers of management together in ways they might not have prior to GPRA.

Additionally, incongruent policy objectives between old and new political leadership can be addressed through a formal update of an agency's long-term strategic plan; high-ranking careerists are often central to such updates. This process has the added benefit of clearly and publicly establishing an agency's new policy objectives early in each new administration; in principle, this may strengthen or accelerate productive relationships among these layers of management. GPRA has helped to create a "common language" for careerists and political appointees, helping careerists to communicate a "performance culture" to their new political leaders.

Evidence also demonstrates that the GPRA process is perceived as being "owned" by the careerists, enabling them to approach new politicals with an established management framework to help mobilize and carry out their new policy directives. GPRA's statutory framework provides a level of continuity during political leadership transitions that can be adjusted around the margins to reflect the policy goals and directions of the new administration. Additionally, careerists with well-functioning strategic planning and

performance reporting systems in place are also in a better position to manage for results; that is, the ability to better direct their agencies' budgetary
and human capital resources toward the policy objectives set by their new
political leadership.

Conversely, the PMA is a process that is perceived as being owned by
political appointees. The PMA has helped to drive and sustain agency interest in GPRA—even as congressional interest in GPRA seems to be waning.
More importantly, the PMA's ambitious goal-setting requirements have
helped to sustain a transformation of agency culture inaugurated by GPRA.

Findings Derived from Case Studies

The three case studies of agencies' experiences in implementing both
GPRA and the PMA, and their joint effects on relationships between career
and political executives in a transition of political leadership, yielded a series
of findings that can help new political appointees as they take on the challenges of leadership in a new environment.

**Finding 1. GPRA has created a common language for politicals and
careerists, and this common language offers a number of benefits to the
political/careerist relationship.**

Many interviewees noted that, in the past, it was easy for political
appointees and careerists to operate within their own "parallel universes"
without interacting much with one another. One interviewee suggested
that GPRA, the PMA, and PART—and the process of goal setting and performance measurement that each requires—can create a convergence of
interests by establishing the grounds for a constructive dialogue between
politicals and careerists. Another program director likened careerist/politi-
cal interactions to two college wrestlers who continually circle the mat but
never really engage each other. He added that GPRA is the mechanism that
allows these two individuals to engage each other on a number of issues.

A number of interviewees suggested that data generated from PMA and
GPRA exercises can make it easier for careerists to approach political appointees regarding their policy decisions, if necessary. One interviewee noted
that careerists now have information at their disposal to say, "Hey boss, that's
a great idea, but..." or even "Hey boss, why don't we find another way to
do this because the proposed way *is illegal....*" One specific example of this
type of interaction occurred in HUD during the political leadership transition.
Regarding one program, an early revision of the interim strategic plan did
not include one of the program's core functions as authorized by Congress.
Careerists were able to approach the assistant secretary who oversaw their
program about their concern. One interviewee recounted that he "was able
to go to meetings with the secretary and the other assistant secretaries and

Major Findings

Finding 1:   GPRA has created a common language for politicals and careerists, and this common language offers a number of benefits to the political/careerist relationship.

Finding 2:   The GPRA process helped smooth the transition in political leadership from the Clinton to the Bush administration.

Finding 3:   Updating GPRA required plans to better reflect the policy goals of the new administration during the transition of political leadership was a beneficial exercise and, in principle, has the potential to strengthen or accelerate productive relationships among careerists and political appointees.

Finding 4:   Setting ambitious goals may also help improve relationships.

Finding 5:   The GPRA process is perceived as being "owned" by careerists; however, it is also seen as a tool that can be used to help political leadership advance the goals and policy agenda of the current administration.

Finding 6:   Generally, the political staff tends to be more focused on the President's Management Agenda, and career staff and managers tend to be more GPRA oriented.

Finding 7:   Congressional interest in GPRA may be waning.

Finding 8:   Interviewees in all three agencies reported a positive shift in department culture and internal management practices and generally attributed these shifts to GPRA.

Finding 9:   Under some conditions, the GPRA and PMA process may help to exacerbate tensions between political appointees and career managers.

say, 'Hey, wait a minute, you've left out a large part of the department here.' " The interim strategic plan was then revised to include this core programmatic component, and both political and career interviewees who spoke about this example reported this as a mutually beneficial experience.

Another career interviewee noted that GPRA has caused the discussion between careerists and politicals to be more strategic, has given careerists and political appointees similar tools to manage, and—most importantly—has established "a new managerial discipline" in his agency. Likewise, a political interviewee noted that GPRA-generated performance information helps both politicals and careerists, stating that "anytime you can get solid, measurable results to show people, it removes the skepticism … anytime you can remove

the 'I think' part of the statement, you're going to have a lot more credibility." One interviewee also noted the usefulness of the GPRA framework
for the Bush administration's performance and budget integration initiative
under the PMA, which links program performance to the budgetary process:

> ... before, we used to present our budget in terms of activity mea-
> sures. Now we have to present our budget in terms of what results are
> expected. And that is probably going to be institutionalized. So the
> political folks, they do use a common language to defend their budgets
> in terms of GPRA terminology. So that seems to be a positive effect.

Another benefit of this common language is the formalization and
institutionalization of clear goals and responsibilities. One interviewee
from NASA added:

> I think that GPRA and strategic plans set the framework; they're the road
> map for everything that we do. The vision is very broad and the mission
> even is broad. But, if you can't see what we're doing in there somewhere,
> we ought to be out of that business. So I think that forces—whether you're
> talking career people or career and political—it's a forcing function that
> keeps people on the same page. And whether it helps them work better
> together or more collaboratively ... what I think it does is sets kind of a clear
> road map, so you do not have the divergence that you might have other-
> wise. It just makes things clearer. And from that, I think that you've got more
> clarity in terms of responsibilities and roles and who's doing what.

In contrast, one OSHA interviewee noted a lag between the time program data is collected and the time that it can be used to measure outcomes
(up to 18 months in some cases), and suggested that this lag can sometimes
limit the usefulness of results data for career/political interactions. Given
the short tenure of many political appointees, this lag may prevent some
politicals from evaluating programs initiated during their tenure. Finally,
another interviewee suggested that sometimes performance data can
demonstrate that a program is working too well and that data can be used
to cut politically charged programs in spite of their success. He cited the
example of the Clinton administration's $15 million gun buyback program,
in which HUD distributed monies to local law enforcement agencies to
buy back and destroy guns near federally funded housing projects. Data
suggests that over 20,000 guns were destroyed in the program's first year.
The interviewee suggested that this program was too successful for the new
presidential administration, and the program was subsequently halted by the
Bush administration.

Finding 2. The GPRA process helped smooth the transition in political leadership from the Clinton to the Bush administration.

Although GPRA requires agencies to submit an update to their long-term strategic plan to OMB every three years, many departments and agencies updated their strategic plans early to better reflect the values and policy goals of the Bush administration. Interviewees in each agency generally reported that the updates were a very collaborative process between political appointees and careerists. However, there was some evidence to suggest that the amount of collaboration between politicals and careerists also varied by office or program, and at times there may have been less substantive involvement by the career staff in the strategic planning updates.

An interviewee from HUD suggested that the planning process created by GPRA is the most important part of smoothing transitions, as it "connects political will with strategic directions of departments and programs." He added that the process allows careerists and politicals to evaluate policy and program administration all the way to their ultimate goal, and to consider the effects of both "achieving this goal and who is contributing all along the way." Another interviewee suggested that GPRA allows the "communication of a performance culture" to new political appointees.

One program director added that the benefit of GPRA is that it has institutionalized "repeatable transaction cycles" within his agency. He explained that under these cycles, an underlying management structure is present when new political leadership assumes power. "Road maps" for the agency are in place and careerists are able to adjust them as necessary. With these repeatable transaction cycles, agencies also have increased internal controls and are better able to know what they are currently doing, which allows a "match between what we say we do, and what we in fact do." Finally, a political appointee interviewed suggests that the GPRA process:

> … definitely helps that transition go smoother, because before you had something in place like GPRA, you'd have a political person coming in and a career person telling him that "this is the way we've always done it." And the political person saying that "well, you've been here too long, because this is the way the outside world is doing it—this is how we're going to do it." And you don't have as much of that when you have something like a framework that you have to follow to a certain extent.

Interestingly, interviewees from NASA generally indicated that GPRA was beneficial during the transition, but were somewhat more mixed as to the extent to which it contributed to smoothing the transition. A few of these interviewees suggested that NASA was less political than other agencies, with only four Senate-confirmed political appointees and seven Schedule C appointees. Moreover, NASA's latest administrator was appointed and confirmed over 11 months into the Bush administration. Regarding the transition, one NASA interviewee suggested that:

> ... having the systems, or the process—the requirements to have certain things in place helped with the transition, but we started anew when Sean O'Keefe came. And I would suspect when he leaves that there will probably be a similar kind of effort. But, it does ensure some continuity because our work ... is not just short-term programs and projects. They are multiyear—space exploration and aeronautics technology and things like that. So while somebody can come in and change some of the direction based on a new strategic plan or a new strategic vision and mission, you don't just start canning things you've made a significant investment in. So I think it's a helpful thing, and I think there is enough flexibility in the system to allow continuity but at the same time give flexibility to allow new leadership to be able to do what they believe needs to be done in the agency using the GPRA process.

Finding 3. Updating GPRA required plans to better reflect the policy goals of the new administration during the transition of political leadership was a beneficial exercise and, in principle, has the potential to strengthen or accelerate productive relationships among careerists and political appointees.

Arguably, long-term strategic planning promotes continuity and stability between changes in political leadership and can help depoliticize agency management. However, during the transition from Clinton to Bush, the new political leadership in many agencies updated their long-term strategic goals and revised many of their performance report measurements to better reflect the policy objectives of the new administration. This was accomplished through the provision of GPRA that requires agencies to update their strategic plans every three years (though in all cases the update occurred before the third year). Interviews reveal that, in principle, this process of revising and updating GPRA requirements may help accelerate productive working relationships.

First, there is an existing management framework in place, which provides an institutionalized means for careerists and politicals to reach out to each other early during the transition. One political appointee noted that this is true:

> ... to the extent that the political lead is savvy enough to understand how he or she is going to treat everyone on day one. Some people will come in and say, "Now there's a new sheriff in town, and I don't care what you've done before—things are going to be different." And not really appreciating the fact that it takes a long time to reinvent the wheel. Take the wheel that is there and fix it. Some are savvy enough to know that "I've only got 18 months in order for me to be successful; I've got to get key people on board with my vision."

Second, to the extent that revisions are a collaborative effort between political appointees and career managers, this process brings career managers and political appointees together early regarding policy-related matters. Additionally, incongruent policy objectives between the old and new political leadership can be addressed through a formal update of the agency's long-term strategic plan; high-level careerists are often central to such updates. This process has the added benefit of clearly and publicly establishing the policy objectives and expectations of new political leadership.

Agency interviews also revealed that this process might help accelerate the learning curve for political appointees. One political appointee pointed out that any new political leadership must learn to negotiate a number of administrative, legislative, and political constraints that agencies face over the budgetary process. Arguably, the performance information generated by GPRA and the extent to which political appointees tap the expertise of careerists can help them learn to negotiate these constraints. Another career interviewee suggested that this process benefits both politicals and careerists:

> ... the current administration came in and dealt with the previous strategic plan, but then said all right, and came up with an interim strategic plan, and modified all of the indicators in the annual performance plan. So I think it helps both. The politicals have a better idea of what the programs are doing to see these concrete indicators and then that helps them focus with a clear vision of what they want ... the direction that they want to go. I think it helps everyone say, "Oh, this is what we are aiming to do."

More generally, one interviewee in HUD noted that GPRA gives careerists and politicals a number of "mutually interrelated objectives" to address. At the very least, he suggested that these statutory objectives can help encourage reasonable working relationships between politicals and careerists. He added that for the new political leaders, there is a "law about HUD, a law about what is expected about HUD and all federal agencies," which allows careerists and politicals to look for opportunities. They can tweak strategic goals, find common ground, and help the president achieve his policies, "all under the context of HUD." Finally, he added that a "big plus" of GPRA is the "state of rapport, cooperation, and understanding" that was not present prior to GPRA.

Thus, any process that helps streamline or reduce the adjustment period could help solidify these relationships earlier and subsequently reduce tensions in the long run. With this said, it is possible that GPRA requirements could also help reduce barriers between careerists and politicals by bringing these two layers of management together in the pursuit of superordinate departmental goals.

Finding 4. Setting ambitious goals may also help improve relationships.

Interview data also suggest that the formalized process of goal setting under GPRA—and to some extent the current efforts of the PMA—might help build a foundation to foster productive working relationships between political appointees and careerists, especially where setting ambitious goals is concerned. One interviewee suggested that ambitious goal setting increases dialogue and promotes cooperation between politicals and careerists. Good career program managers can help with this by recognizing crosscutting goals and leveraging agencies with similar goals and stakeholders (and in many cases quasi-government entities) toward the fulfillment of that goal. This interviewee also noted that when confronted with ambitious goals, "necessity is the mother of all invention," and politicals and careerists often find innovative means to achieve these goals.

Through the PMA, the Bush administration and HUD's political leadership set two ambitious but attainable goals: increasing minority homeownership by 5.5 million units and eliminating chronic homelessness in 10 years. Career and political interviewees indicated that these ambitious goals brought workers together, energized them, and got them excited to achieve these goals. One HUD political appointee noted that the PMA scorecard also helps to inject a healthy dose of competition between agency programs and across similar agencies, stating that these programs "want to be the first to get to green." Another interviewee stated that ambitious goal setting:

> … speaks to better government—a federal government that is making a difference. I think there is a lot said about creating goals that are loftier than what you are accustomed to. It does create an incentive for greater cooperation internally, because goals are set at a level that requires you to stretch yourself higher than your comfort zone in just getting the job done—punching in and punching out. But setting higher goals creates that synergy for greater cooperation internally.

Finally, another appointee added that ambitious or visionary goal setting has the potential to promote comity between politicals and careerists to the extent that they both agree with the overarching goal. He cited HUD's goal to end chronic homelessness within 10 years and stated that HUD's efforts toward this nonpartisan goal have made significant changes in the way homelessness is now addressed across the nation—and especially by federal, state, and local government agencies. In contrast, this interviewee suggested that ambitious partisan goals may not promote the same degree of comity or relationship-building potential among politicals and careerists.

Finding 5. The GPRA process is perceived as being "owned" by careerists; however, it is also seen as a tool that can be used to help political leadership advance the goals and policy agenda of the current administration.

Several interviewees suggested that GPRA is a process that is owned by the careerists, and another interviewee likened GPRA to a "constitution" for career managers to carry out their agency's mission and offered the following observation:

> GPRA, with its focus on performance, gave the public servant the ability to rise up and say, "OK, I'm a public servant being held to account for performance, and this is what it will take for me to perform." Then if the agency or the Congress wants to say "no," then that's perfectly all right because the process has worked. But at least the public servant has had a chance to stand up and say "this is what it will take to run this program in the best way." Whereas during that period of across-the-board prorated cuts, if you proposed anything other than simply taking your cut and saluting, you were on the verge of losing your job or severely damaging your career. So I say that the law has had—and can have—an even stronger effect on the concept of management.

Some interviewees suggested that, through the managerial tools set forth by GPRA, it is possible for careerists to increase their responsiveness to politicals in fulfillment of the department's core missions. This observation is also supported by a 2004 Government Accountability Office (GAO) finding that suggests "within agencies, GPRA documents can provide a context of missions, goals, and strategies that political appointees can use to articulate agencies' priorities." One career interviewee added that:

> … we do have a better idea of where the politicals want to go, by going through the process of developing their overall goals, and, of course, we sort of fill in the words. But it does allow us to get a better sense. For example, the previous administration had a very strong focus on economic development. If you look at our strategic plan that was done a year ago—the latest one—there's not a strategic objective for economic development. So clearly in this administration that is not as much of a focus.

However, another interviewee was very careful to note that while the process resides with the careerists, the goals attached to the process ultimately reside with the political staff (but still within the parameters of the department's general mission). To the extent that political appointees and careerists work within the parameters of GPRA, these tools can be a force that can promote cooperative management.

Finding 6. Generally, the political staff tends to be more focused on the President's Management Agenda, and career staff and managers tend to be more GPRA oriented.

The PMA is the primary vehicle of the Bush administration to manage to its policy objectives, so it is reasonable for political appointees to focus on this aspect of agency management. Additionally, many career interviewees suggested that political appointees were less concerned with GPRA minutiae than its overall results and that the PMA and PART were the primary managerial focus by politicals in all three agencies. For instance, NASA has a team leader for each of the five PMA management areas, and team leaders meet weekly with the administrator to report on their team's progress toward their PMA goals.

Interviewees also characterized GPRA and the PMA very differently. One interviewee characterized GPRA as capacity building and the PMA as a tool to realize short-term political goals. Another interviewee attributed GPRA's focus to good government and long-term achievable milestones and attributed the PMA's focus to episodic milestones and tangible, achievable goals. (Yet another interviewee characterized PMA goals as résumé builders for political appointees.) Generally interviewees reported that PMA and GPRA goals generally complemented each other or built off of one another at both the program and agency or department levels. Often PMA goals were incorporated into the overall goal-setting framework established by GPRA in each agency. One interviewee characterized the PMA and PART as follows:

> PART is a piece of the PMA. The PMA is performance, results-based management. Everything they try and do is to become more efficient, more effective, and that's really the foundation of the five management areas. With the PMA, there is stuff that you try and do, but that is being handled at a much broader level. So it doesn't affect you as rapidly as it does if you're working for a program.

Interestingly, career interviewees who work closely with GPRA suggest that the potential for career/political tensions exists between the President's Management Agenda, the OMB's Program Assessment Rating Tool, or PART, and GPRA. Interviewees reported that career staff and managers are becoming burdened by the voluminous amount of time and paperwork that goes into GPRA, PMA, and PART compliance, and noted the potential for competing goals, measurements, and lines of accountability between the three initiatives. One political appointee described the process surrounding a PART review:

> So eight months ago they said, "Hey, this year's PART analysis they're doing [program name withheld]. Well, as soon as they say that, you're getting a consultant, because you need someone in the office who can focus totally on PART. Because you need to get all of your reporting stuff together, because the way they want to see the information may not be the way that you have the information and what they want. You may do it, but you have to get it into their format to give it to them to prove that's what you do.

The PART is much more stressful, because everyone realizes it's tied into your money line. With PART, you're defending your program, and that's the difference. The other PMA stuff is just adjustments to how you are doing things to make it more efficient. PART is where they are actually saying to you: "You know what, you tell me ... you show me that your program works. Don't tell me about it, but show me it works, and then we'll give you money." So there is much more pressure.

Many interviewees described PART as a "painful" process. Although the PMA and PART are examples of executive-based management reform efforts, one interviewee stated that he felt that they have both made significant inroads into agency culture that would probably survive the Bush administration.

Finding 7. Congressional interest in GPRA may be waning.

A few interviewees felt that the information that their department generated for its GPRA requirement went relatively unnoticed by Congress. This "waning" may be due in part to a shift in priorities for the Senate Committee on Governmental Affairs and the House Committee on Governmental Reform. Indeed, until his retirement in 2000, Senator Fred Thompson chaired the Senate Committee on Governmental Affairs, championed GPRA, and was quite vociferous regarding GPRA oversight. One interviewee felt that congressional interests and agency involvement would continue to wane without such an outspoken proponent. However, a number of interviewees from HUD noted that some congressional committees and subcommittees that oversee HUD and its programs frequently make use of HUD planning and performance information generated by GPRA.

Interviewees offered a range of views regarding the current state of GPRA within these agencies. One interviewee who worked very closely on GPRA's implementation and oversight felt that GPRA was fading out in favor of the President's Management Agenda, although an interviewee from the Department of Labor suggested that the PMA has helped to sustain and give new life to GPRA. In spite of sporadic and sometimes episodic interest or support from Congress, virtually all interviewees articulated that GPRA-mandated processes (but often with the exception of the workload it entails) have made a difference and are eminently beneficial to overall agency management. Interviewees generally reported that the processes mandated by GPRA were very much a part of current government and agency culture, and many suggested that they would continue many of the practices set by GPRA if GPRA requirements were to cease.

Parenthetically, two interviewees who worked with the drafting of GPRA suggested that the extent to which GPRA is fading marks the extent of its success—claiming that its intellectual founders felt they could claim success if the acronym faded from the lexicon, but the statutory requirements remained entrenched in government agency culture. These interviewees added that the Bush administration's PMA would not be possible without the solid groundwork set by GPRA in the areas of defining missions, setting strategic goals, and measuring performance.

One problem associated with waning congressional interest is the potential for GPRA compliance to degenerate into a mere paperwork exercise. This could become a source of tension between careerists and politicals if GPRA becomes a compliance exercise and the departmental operations begin to deviate or "creep" from departmental missions and goals established per GPRA. Additionally, tensions between careerists and politicals may increase if competing goals and performance measures exist between executive reform efforts and GPRA. However, another program director noted that even if congressional interest is waning, GPRA-generated performance and outcome information is utilized "when public interests representing their clients for state and local governments go to testify on the Hill about our effectiveness."

Finding 8. Interviewees in all three agencies reported a positive shift in department culture and internal management practices and generally attributed these shifts to GPRA.

Many interviewees suggested that GPRA acted as a mechanism to compel them to review and revise their management practices. A few interviewees confided that, initially, GPRA was viewed as "another flavor of the month" and not taken very seriously, but noted that the overall process of developing and honing strategic plans and performance measurement systems has been beneficial to overall agency management. Indeed, one NASA careerist stated:

> ... and that's one of the positive sides of all of this; it drove us to think about longer-term outcome goals. Because we certainly had to think in terms of what are we really doing in the long run, what kind of knowledge are we basically trying to achieve 10 years out.... And every year we'll come back and evaluate internally our progress against the road map that we've bought into with our stakeholders and the OMB and Congress and everybody else.

A career interviewee within HUD characterized the shift as very positive and asserted that GPRA has brought a new discipline to HUD management that is based on the annual budget. Another HUD interviewee characterized the overall agency culture as "slow moving and bureaucratic," but suggested that GPRA has helped to streamline certain aspects of management. Moreover, an interviewee from NASA added that:

> ... another area it's been useful is that it's been a forcing mechanism to really take the strategic planning process seriously. And our strategic planning activity is rather intensive in terms of getting our community on board and how our strategic plan has a tie-in with our longer-term goals. We can better manage internally and know how the science questions we're

pursuing and the dollars that can be attributed—not at specific targets in any enforceable measure but at the macro level. So there is a relationship now that we feel more comfortable having dollars tied to the outcomes and annual goals and long-term outcome goals.

Finding 9. Under some conditions, the GPRA and PMA process may help to exacerbate tensions between political appointees and career managers.

Interviewees suggested that at times the sheer volume of compliance activities for GPRA, PART, and the PMA could increase tensions between politicals and careerists. One interviewee noted that a significant amount of her time and resources was devoted to meeting requirements and that these resources may be better allocated elsewhere.

Additionally, one political noted that agencies have "dictates from multiple masters"—for example, the Hill, other agencies, the executive branch, OMB, and political appointees. Thus, GPRA and PMA compliance also has the potential to place careerists at odds with any one of these organizations.

GPRA, PMA, and most performance management systems are predicated on the idea that performance information will inform the budgetary process. In theory, this process should remain apolitical. However, one interviewee explained that politics creeps into this process and that natural tensions between political appointees and career managers can result, especially when careerists are caught in the middle of executive and legislative budgetary conflicts. For instance, PART links program performance to the budgetary process; programs that meet performance goals should see increased budgets and poor performers should see budgetary cuts. However, he suggested that politicals might not fully understand that "you cannot fully avoid the congressional part" of the budgetary process. Tensions can arise when programs favored by the executive branch are cut by Congress or when programs that are cut by the executive branch are restored by Congress. In the first example, careerists must continue to execute the program despite a reduction in available resources; in the second example, careerists must continue to faithfully execute a program that their political bosses may not really care about.

Conclusions

The interviews conducted for this study suggest that the results-oriented managerial reforms embodied in GPRA and the PMA have helped to mitigate historic tensions between political appointees and career civil servants by creating a common ground around achieving mission results. Since many of these perennial tensions stem from long-standing differences in perspectives, they are not easily reconciled. Indeed, a long litany of previous administrative reform efforts has largely been ineffectual in reconciling these relationships. However, the statutory basis and longevity of GPRA—and subsequent supporting efforts in the PMA—have helped to change agency culture and institutionalize many of the tenets of performance management in the federal workplace. Moreover, the Bush administration's emphasis on the PMA has helped breathe new life into GPRA. According to many interviewees in this study, it is also likely that aspects of the PMA, including current efforts to connect performance reporting to the budgetary process, will become institutionalized and will survive the Bush administration.

The performance-oriented frameworks offered by GPRA and PMA afford career managers and political appointees many opportunities to reach across the bureaucratic divide to focus on common objectives—getting results Americans care about. Indeed, the most important lessons are those which help to accelerate mutually beneficial working relationships by smoothing the often stressful transition of political leadership, creating a common language for career managers and political appointees, and promoting more substantively meaningful policy making by increasing collaboration between these two executive-branch actors.

Acknowledgments

Funds were generously provided by the IBM Center for The Business of Government and a Maxwell Dissertation Fellowship. The author would like to acknowledge Patricia Ingraham, Suzanne Mettler, and Dale Jones for their support and advice, especially during the early stages of this project. Heartfelt thanks and appreciation go out to Rogan Kersh for his unremitting guidance and superb contributions over the course of the project. Finally, the author wishes to express gratitude to all of the career staff and managers, political appointees, and performance management experts for their participation in the project. Ultimately, any errors or omissions in the project remain the sole responsibility of the author.

CHAPTER EIGHT

Performance Management for Political Executives: A "Start Where You Are, Use What You Have" Guide

Chris Wye

This report was originally published in October 2004.

Introduction

Listening at the Front Lines

I was sitting at a table listening to a focus group identify the top challenges facing those charged with implementing the Government Performance and Results Act (GPRA). A professional facilitator was guiding the discussion; an assistant was recording the comments on a flip chart.

The group was not very engaged, and the comments were fairly ordinary. Some sounded like complaints: "We don't have the staff." "No one uses this stuff." "Our managers are not engaged."

Then someone said, "You know, our leader—the secretary—isn't interested in GPRA." Someone else said, "Same here." Another: "So, what's new?" And the dialogue took off: "You know, if anyone really wants this stuff to work, top leaders, especially the top political leaders, need to get engaged."

"And mean it," someone added.

A decade after the enactment of the Government Performance and Results Act, it is still clear—as it has been through the entire period regardless of the party in power—that political leaders have not really taken the act as seriously as they should.

It seems strange.

The law requires agencies to have a strategic plan, to establish performance goals and measures, and to report performance on an annual basis.

Isn't that what citizens should expect from the government that manages their tax dollars? And, as the top leaders in this government, directly accountable to the voting public, are not political appointees the ones most directly accountable for performance?

Everyone—not "almost everyone" or "practically everyone" but literally everyone—who has assessed progress under GPRA has come to the conclusion that top leaders, by and large, do not take it as seriously as they should, and because they don't the program managers who report to them don't take it as seriously as they should.

The most recent review of progress under GPRA, the Government Accountability Office's "Results-Oriented Government" (March 2004) concluded: "As we have noted before, top leadership commitment and sustained attention to achieving results ... is essential to GPRA implementation. While one might expect an increase in agency leadership commitment since GPRA was implemented ... federal managers reported that such commitment has not significantly increased."

Despite protestations to the contrary and specific initiatives— such as the President's Management Agenda and the emergence of the Program Assessment Rating Tool—everyone (career civil servants, politi-

Author's Note

Strong emphasis is placed in this chapter on the relationship between performance and public service. From this perspective, performance is public service.

For both career and political civil servants, a primary motivation for public service is performance: the desire to make things better for all citizens.

In recent years, a number of pieces of legislation—such as the Government Performance and Results Act, which requires agencies to have strategic plans, annual plans, and annual reports focused on performance measures—have been put in place to help focus management's attention on performance.

In the same period, both political parties have sponsored performance-based management initiatives. President Clinton established the National Performance Review; President George W. Bush, the President's Management Agenda. Doubtless, others will follow.

But these initiatives have not always been implemented as effectively as they might be, and the goal of improved performance gets bogged down in and obscured by counterweights.

In the case of career civil servants, cynicism, discouragement, and weariness can be the cause. In the case of political appointees, sole focus on the political agenda can take undue precedence over fundamental management responsibilities.

Political appointees are first American citizens, second public servants, and third members of a political party.

It would seem that performance—the best performance—would be the natural goal of both political parties. And if the proof were to be found in rhetoric, the country would be awash in "good performance."

But the truth is that for many political appointees, good performance (in the sense of good management) is less a goal in itself but something that is pursued to avoid potential political problems.

Some seem to feel that career public servants have the primary responsibility for management, while political leaders bear primary responsibility for policy and politics. There is some truth to this. Career public servants are professional managers. Many have long tenure and substantial experience in their fields.

But the most important management decisions are made by political leaders. What new management systems should be developed? How much money should be assigned to what activities?

Management at its best and highest is leadership: setting priorities, allocating resources, tracking and achieving results, being accountable.

Performance-based management is nothing more than setting goals and tracking results.

It's allocating money and seeing what it buys—or delivers to American citizens.

It's their money.

Not ours. Not this or that administration's.

Most political appointees, like most career civil servants, want to do a good job. They are proud to be serving their country. They want to leave a good record. They want to make things better.

They just don't spend enough time on performance goals and measures.

cal appointees, interest groups, oversight functions, knowledgeable citizens, and program beneficiaries) believes that top leaders are not doing what they should (and could) to lead the implementation of performance-based management.

Do top executives have a more fundamental responsibility than the performance of their agency, program, or activity? Is this responsibility more or less because the executive is a public servant? Is this responsibility more or less because the executive is a political appointee?

The Issues on the Ground

The purpose of this chapter is to respond to some of the most frequently heard comments made by political appointees about GPRA and other related performance-based management issues on the ground.

The intent is to provide direct answers to questions, antidotes to discouragement, practical suggestions to solve problems, and, most of all, to highlight the obligation all political appointees have to render the best and highest service—performance—to their country and its citizens.

As the former director of the Center for Improving Government Performance at the National Academy of Public Administration, I had the opportunity to see and hear many of the leading experts and practitioners in performance-based management from this and many other countries.

And, as the former director of the Center's Performance Consortium—a membership organization made up of 30 federal agencies that fund an annual program of peer-to-peer exchange of practices—I had the opportunity to meet and get to know many of the people involved in the implementation of the Results Act.

Members of the consortium normally were not the managers of programs or political leaders. They were the civil servants charged with preparing and submitting required plans and reports. Their work brought them into contact with the political appointees responsible for performance management issues. Typically, these were deputy assistant secretaries, some were assistant secretaries, and a few were deputy or undersecretaries.

It is the views of these political appointees as reflected in the comments of career civil servants who worked for them that are the focus of this chapter. The issues are framed as they were reported—in the vernacular: "GPRA Is Just Paperwork," "Performance Management Is a Fad," "The Private Sector Is Different," "Congress Is Not Interested."

The issues have been culled from meetings, reports, workshops, and conferences sponsored by the Performance Consortium, as well as from conversations with individual consortium members—all over a 10-year period. The responses also have been taken from this dialogue.

The formulation of neither the issues nor the responses as presented here represents a consensus or official view. The author alone is solely responsible for both.

A Few Answers Resolve Many Questions

This chapter responds to a long list of issues, all of which are expressed in short phrases, as they would occur in daily conversation. Each issue is presented as a statement in bold at the top of the page. The text that follows presents contextual background and analysis, and concludes with several recommended responses.

The chapter is not meant to be read serially. If it is read from start to finish, it will be found to be repetitive. It is meant to be used as a reference to locate responses—or, more properly, to prompt dialogue and jump-start thought and discussion—in relation to particular issues. The recommended responses given are intended as illustrative. Others can easily be imagined.

Repetition is unavoidable. The concept of performance management is not complex; it is not rocket science. We may pose many questions and define many issues, but most can be addressed with a relatively small number of responses.

The central principles of performance-based management are the same for political appointees as for career civil servants. Both are *public servants.*

But there is one very important difference, and that difference is at the heart of what this chapter is all about: As the highest-level leaders, political appointees have the highest level of responsibility for performance.

So, while the core principles for performance management are the same for both career and political appointees, appointees—being the top leaders—have the highest level of responsibility.

The following is a list of core performance management principles that reflect this higher level of responsibility:

- **Political appointees have the highest level of leadership responsibility** for assuming responsibility as individual public servants for the high trust inherent in their calling.
- **Political appointees have the highest level of leadership responsibility** for searching continuously for the highest-quality public service at the lowest cost.
- **Political appointees have the highest level of leadership responsibility** for using creatively whatever information can be found to improve programs.
- **Political appointees have the highest level of leadership responsibility** for doing something (to improve performance) in the face of all obstacles, as opposed to doing nothing.

- **Political appointees have the highest level of leadership responsibility** for placing boundaries on discouragement and moving constantly toward the high and noble goal of public service.
- **Political appointees have the highest level of leadership responsibility** for remembering that the money supporting public endeavors is not theirs but the public's, and that they are the trustees.

Neither career nor noncareer civil servants can promise or deliver perfect performance-based management. Management, almost by definition, is the art of the possible. Resources are scarce. Time is short. People are busy. No appropriation was made to support the implementation of the Government Performance and Results Act or most of the related performance-based initiatives.

But between doing nothing and doing everything, *something can be done.*

And, even with limited resources, some will do more and better than others. A few will do exceptional things.

Doing nothing or doing something with weak intent is not acceptable.

American citizens deserve your best effort.

Why Should Political Leaders Care about Performance Management?

Political leaders are triply vested—as American citizens, appointed public servants, and members of an incumbent political party—with bottom-line responsibility for the performance of the policies, programs, and activities entrusted to their care. During their term in office, no other category of citizens carries a higher and more sovereign mission or holds a clearer and more complete responsibility for the performance of government.

The *only* way political leaders can reliably know whether the resources and activities entrusted to their care are being managed efficiently and effectively, having the desired impact, and providing the highest possible quality service—in short, improving government performance—is through *vigilant monitoring of information about performance*. In today's world, this responsibility is called *performance management*. Its central requirement is that there be sufficient, credible, useful, and timely information about the effects of government activities so as to assure full accountability, thus preserving the integrity of both the American democratic political process and the government through which its priorities are established and carried out.

Organization of the Chapter

This chapter is organized into five major sections. These are presented in the order in which the issues would arise in everyday practice.

The first section, "Making the Case for Performance Management," considers some of the objections and less-than-enthusiastic attitudes sometimes expressed toward the Results Act and related performance-based management initiatives. The next four sections take up specific stages in the design, installation, use, and communication of performance management techniques: "Designing Performance Indicators," "Aligning Performance Processes," "Using Performance Information," and "Communicating Performance Information." Each section discusses a number of specific issues. The format is the same for each discussion. Each begins with a statement in bold, followed by a discussion of the issue and concludes with several recommended responses.

Making the Case for Performance Management

Ten years ago, few incoming political appointees knew much about "performance management."

Fewer still knew about the Government Performance and Results Act.

Today, many new appointees know something about performance-based management because they have either heard about it or had direct experience with it in the private sector.

They may learn about GPRA and related performance initiatives for the first time when they arrive in Washington, but their previous experience often prepares them to understand its basic concepts. They also understand that performance-based management techniques are being pursued in both the private and public sectors all over the world.

Sometimes, too, they bring with them the view that the concepts of "public service" and "performance" are incongruous, that "the Washington bureaucracy" does not or cannot perform at the highest level.

Sometimes they see the work that has been done to date under GPRA and other performance initiatives as less than perfect and as a confirmation that the bureaucracy just can't hack it.

Almost always they conclude their terms of service and leave Washington with a very different—and much more positive—view toward the civil service.

Recent Presidential Management Initiatives

In recent years, presidents of both political parties have pursued a "reform" agenda aimed at improving the management of government.

1993–2001
President Bill Clinton:
The National Performance Review

The National Performance Review (NPR)—later called the National Partnership for Reinventing Government—was led by Vice President Al Gore. NPR conducted a six-month review of the federal government, which provided the basis for hundreds of recommendations for improving performance by cutting the size of the workforce, eliminating management layers, and adopting performance-based management, and for changing the culture of the government. Under the leadership of NPR, cabinet agencies empowered reinvention teams, reinvention laboratories, experimentation, and cultural change by proposing new approaches, collecting useful examples, and launching demonstration projects.

2001–2004
President George W. Bush:
The President's Management Agenda
The Program Assessment Rating Tool

The President's Management Agenda (PMA) is intended to encourage a performance-based approach to management by identifying key priorities and closely tracking their performance. The PMA focuses on five priorities: the strategic management of human capital, competitive sourcing, financial management, electronic government, and budget and performance integration. Each initiative is coordinated by a government-wide leader, and all initiatives are monitored through a scorecard that assigns a red, yellow, or green light to indicate unacceptable, minimally acceptable, and outstanding performance.

The Program Assessment Rating Tool (PART) is an effort to leverage greater attention to performance-based management by using the budget to establish an effective link between the quality of information available on the performance of an activity or program and the level of resources devoted to that activity or program. The PART is a fill-in-the-blank survey designed to answer questions about four broad topics: program purpose and design, strategic planning, program management, and program results. Answers are scored, and a total score is given for each activity or program. The PART process is data centric: Success or failure, as evident in higher or lower overall scores, depends on the data (read "information on performance") available to answer each question.

A Primer on Recent Management Reform Legislation

The last decade and a half has given rise to a spate of legislation aimed at improving the performance of government. Key pieces of legislation include the following:

1990: The Chief Financial Officers (CFO) Act
Intended to strengthen financial accountability in the government, the CFO Act created chief financial officers in the largest federal agencies who are responsible for managing agency financial matters, required the Office of Management and Budget (OMB) to develop a five-year financial plan and report for the government, and required agency CFOs to conform their financial plans to the government-wide plan.

1993: The Government Performance and Results Act (GPRA)
The centerpiece of recent performance legislation, GPRA requires agencies to set goals and measure performance toward them. Each agency must prepare a three-year strategic plan, an annual plan, and an annual report. OMB is required to prepare a government-wide plan. A unique feature of GPRA is its strong focus on outcome measures.

1994: The Government Management and Reform Act (GMRA)
Designed to strengthen the CFO Act, GMRA extended the act by requiring an audit of each agency's financial statement as well as of the government-wide financial statement.

1996: The Information Technology Management Reform Act (ITMRA)
Also known as the Clinger-Cohen Act, ITMRA created the position of chief information officer in the largest federal agencies. CIOs are required to implement a "sound and integrated information technology architecture." The act empowers OMB to issue directives to CIOs, effectively giving OMB a leadership and coordinating responsibility position.

1996: The Federal Financial Management Improvement Act (FFMIA)
Again tightening the screws on agency financial management, FFMIA requires that agency annual financial statements include a report showing where their financials are in compliance with federal financial requirements, accounting standards, and the U.S. Government Standard General Ledger.

1998: Government Paperwork Elimination Act (GPEA)
Intended to encourage the use of electronic, Web-based applications, the GPEA requires agencies to offer an electronic option for information gathering or use, and also requires agencies to accept electronic signatures.

"The Private Sector Is Different"

It is different.

But *difference* is not the point being made. The point often being made is that it's *better* in the private sector.

How many times has this remark been made, or something like it? And how many times has the intended point been difference?

You would think that over a period of time, say four or five decades, this kind of remark would be so embarrassing to its originator—and would reveal so much lack of thought, knowledge, professionalism, and courtesy—that it would cease to be made, at least not for public consumption.

Indeed, if difference were really the issue, the case can be made in reverse.

Government, and especially the United States government, is different from the private sector. It presides over the largest, most complex, most successful economy in the world, and at the same time delivers an amazing array of social services to a wide range of citizens.

Benchmarked against other governments, it's among the best in many areas.

We sometimes forget that the U.S. government is the largest human organization on the planet, dwarfing firms like General Electric and Microsoft. Bigness brings management challenges unknown in the private sector. Just communicating a policy throughout organizations as large as the Departments of Health and Human Services or Defense can take a significant amount of time.

Large organizations do not move as quickly or efficiently as small organizations. Complex organizations are not as nimble as less complex ones. And, in particular, multi-purpose organizations often do not convert resources into services as efficiently as single-purpose organizations.

A profit-oriented bottom line is not simple. But it is simpler than a bottom line whose goal is social equity. Private industry serves some of the people (those who can afford its services). Government must serve all of the people.

The government is not perfect. There's plenty that needs to be done to make it better.

But difference is not the issue.

Recommended Responses

1. It would be useful for individuals who have spent their careers in the private sector to spend some time learning about the government before coming to Washington. Unfortunately, there is no truly effective mechanism in place to assist a new presidential administration as it takes over the reins of power. One of the great unwritten stories of American democracy is what happens—or does not happen—during a transition. Literally, the outgoing administration takes everything that is not bolted to the floor, and the incoming administration has

to start from scratch. But reading, listening, and learning would be a good start.

2. Political leaders should manifest the same level of courtesy, professionalism, and respect in their government positions as they do in their private sector jobs. Not only is this basic humanity, but it is basic management and basic leadership.

"We're Gonna Get It Done"

Less heard than felt, these words reflect an attitude.

When a new administration takes office, a new group of people appears in town, and some are easily identified by their behavior.

"Like I was telling the secretary ...," remarks one new arrival confiding to another. "We've got some big-ticket items over here ...," announces the new chief financial officer at an executive staff meeting, in a tone of voice that conveys disdain for past lack of progress and fervent conviction that it's going to get done *this time around!*

There's an attitude in the air.

It's pervasive. Not everywhere, but pervasive.

It seems so odd. Imagine a newly arrived political appointee who is assigned to coach the Chicago Bulls and is overheard by the team making one of these remarks.

Why would a newly arrived executive in any setting, whether the setting is familiar or not, do anything but try to win over new employees? To turn an old saw around: Would they do it this way in the private sector?

Well, of course, things are more complicated than this. Political appointees, like civil servants, are public servants—and there are an awful lot of good ones.

But the attitude remains and is renewed every time there is a change of administration. And if the attitude is hard to fathom, so is the logic.

The average appointee has a tenure of 18 to 24 months. This is a widely known fact. What could anyone expect to do in a time frame that short without the active help of subordinates?

Conceding that politics is politics, that running against Washington is an effective political strategy, and even that "reorganizing" or "downsizing" the government is a legitimate goal—why would an outnumbered, outpositioned, and outknowledged general antagonize the troops he has to lead into battle?

It's a strange tango.

Especially since many of these same political appointees will leave office with good words to say about their civil service staff, and many civil servants will reluctantly say goodbye to good political leaders.

Recommended Responses

1. Stories are reported and books are written about fabled private sector executives who take over an ailing business, make tough decisions, throw out the deadwood, and get things moving. There is always a need for tough decision making and tough management. But toughness is not the normative or exclusive criteria for effective management, especially when there are more of them than there are of you, and they all know more about the operation than you do. A hard, realistic assessment of the human dimensions of a political transition, and the development of an effective strategy for maximizing the ability to mobilize management resources, would be an enormous benefit.

2. A highly professional, respectful, and courteous manner costs nothing and gains much. It's the same in many walks of life; a little sugar goes a long way. An example of a rare and useful courtesy: Look at the résumés of the people working for you. Almost no one does. You may find some very well-educated and accomplished people, people you'd be proud to have working for you. At a minimum, you'll know who they are.

"We Don't *Need* the Best"

Or words to this effect, said one prominent official, implying that if we just had people who would show up on time and do what they are told, we'd be a lot better off.

This would have been an unfortunate remark for any executive, but it was especially unfortunate because the person making it in 1981 was the director of the Office of Personnel Management, the organization responsible for human resource policy government-wide.

Those who were around when this remark was made will know that these were not the exact words used. There's no need to pin the tail on the donkey, or in this case elephant. But the general attitude conveyed is more widespread, especially at the beginning of a new administration, than is publicly recognized.

The appropriateness (not to mention the effect on morale) of this kind of remark needs no elaboration.

But the question of whether it is true needs to be answered.

Do we or do we not need the best people in public service?

Here are some questions that may help to frame the answer. As a citizen, whom do you want to be responsible for:

*   Protecting the country from enemies
*   Assuring that water and food are safe
*   Maintaining the environment
*   Monitoring the quality of new medicines and drugs
*   Regulating airline safety

Do you want the most competent people you can find, or people who will show up and do what they are told?

This is not to ignore the fact that some civil servants may be inefficient, ineffective, or discourteous; or that some may be less efficient, less effective, or less courteous than they should be.

But if the question is what kind of people do you want managing your government and delivering your services, most of us would want the best and brightest, or at least those who are very good.

Recommended Responses
1. Quality is always in order and in season, no matter what the sector. In fact, one could make the case that the highest standards should be in evidence in the public sector, since in our form of government we delegate to the public service activities to be carried out *on our behalf*—in other words, in place of us and for us. Public servants are our alter egos, doing those things we have decided that we do not wish to do ourselves or that we wish to be done explicitly by others.
2. Be careful about what you say in public. In Washington, very little is exempt from press coverage, almost nothing is confidential, and much less than is supposed to be is off the record. The words you use and impression you convey are completely out of your control, once you act.

"We Don't *Have* the Best"

Now we're at the heart of the issue.

It may be the rare person who *says* that we don't *need* the best people in government, as did the director of the Office of Personnel Management in a well-publicized incident some years ago.

But there are many people who believe that we do not *have* the best people in government, and they extend beyond political appointees to the general public.

The image of the lazy, slothful, dull bureaucrat is everywhere. Without much effort (certainly without much thought), a continual stream of negative commentary in every aspect of public life transforms individual civil servants into an unflattering composite image: the *bureaucrat*.

It's understandable. The out party has to run against the in party, uncover poor performance in the incumbent administration, and promise improvement in a new administration.

What isn't understandable is why poor performance, to the extent that it exists, is always attributed to civil servants rather than to their elected and appointed political leaders.

A look at the facts, focusing squarely on the comparative performance of private versus public sector employees, is worthwhile.

In the early 1980s, a survey was conducted that should be required reading for all incoming political appointees.

The survey was designed and carried out at as a learning exercise by students at the George Washington University School of Public Administration under the direction of the chair of its Public Administration Department, Kathryn Newcomer.

It compared the performance of public and private sector workers, and was based on responses from political appointees from both Democratic and Republican administrations.

The survey showed that in every category of job performance, appointees of both parties rated the civil servants who worked for them at least as well as their private sector employees.

If the facts are important, they are already in.

Recommended Responses
1. Since most appointees conclude their service to the government with a reasonably good view of public servants, it would be useful if an effort were made to incubate this more positive view closer to the beginning of their service. This might be done through a bipartisan initiative. It might be an institutional approach—someone or some entity might provide some initial introductory seminars or training. Time could be spent more efficiently in serving the public if less time were spent criticizing the bureaucrats.
2. It is not likely that political campaigns will cease to criticize "the government bureaucracy." But those institutions that are a part of the accountability process, such as the press and interest groups, should do a better job of reminding the public that the government bureaucracy includes *both* civil servants and political appointees.

"GPRA Is Just Paperwork"

There has always been a strain of thinking to the effect that the Government Performance and Results Act is "just a bunch of paperwork."

GPRA, it will be recalled, requires agencies to produce strategic plans, annual plans, and annual reports whose central focus is the use of performance measures to manage progress toward outcomes (results).

Since its enactment, the law has been implemented with varying degrees of enthusiasm by both parties.

It's hard to see why support has been so uneven.

Imagine a president who wakes up one morning and finds that a new law has been delivered to his doorstep requiring every agency to have plans, goals, measures, and reports. One can envision a state of the union message in which reference is made to the progress being made "getting the government under control."

It seems like a win-win—good politics and good management. The law does require some paperwork. It does take some time and resources. The documents produced to date are not perfect. Specific instances of improvement in management or service quality are sometimes elusive.

But the law provides a legal foundation for good management, especially for accountability; much progress has been made since the law's enactment in 1993; and in management terms, the initiative is still relatively young.

Many feel that the implementation of the law is on a reasonable and predictable path and that additional increments of progress will be in direct proportion to the priority given to GPRA.

Much has been achieved. All over the government, a corps of individuals has acquired an understanding of strategic planning, performance measures, and performance-based management. New management systems have been developed, including new budget account structures.

Executive branch program managers and legislative appropriations committees have been slower to respond, but it's their backyard that's getting redone, and enthusiasm can hardly be expected.

Recommended Responses

1. The Government Performance and Results Act is a law. Performance-based management techniques are taking root all over the world. The private sector is ahead of government in many areas. Citizens deserve the best performance that can be delivered. GPRA deserves proactive leadership priority.
2. Political appointees have a responsibility to manage the organizations and programs for which they are responsible—not just to design and implement the incumbent administration's new initiatives and policies. Some part of this management responsibility should go beyond making day-to-day decisions to include improving the management systems themselves. Career civil servants cannot make institutional improvements by themselves; the needed priorities and resources are beyond their reach.

"Performance Management Is a Fad"

It may be.

But if it is, it's been around a long time, it's all over the world, and it's in the private sector as well.

In the United States, it began in earnest at the federal level in 1993 with the passage of the Government Performance and Results Act. But we were by no means the first to get into it. The governments of Australia, New Zealand, and Canada began much earlier. Great Britain got into it in a substantial way. And today governments as diverse as those in Hong Kong, Singapore, France, and Germany, as well as countries in South and Central America, are engaged.

Sometimes called performance management, performance-based management, performance measurement, or just results-based management, a performance orientation is emerging all over the world.

It appears to be part of an emerging trend in which economic competition among nations and companies, supported by advances in communication and information technology, is creating a global market base in which performance is both an enabler and a driver.

As different parts of the world are drawn together in the economic system, there is a need for a common business language in which fundamental concepts of accountability, efficiency, and quality are known and adhered to. In some parts of the world, such a language does not exist. In order for the economic resources of these areas to enter the world market, they must learn to speak this language.

Similar pressure is being felt by the public sector. Governments all over the world—though they may have the added responsibility of dealing with issues of social policy, social equity, and social service delivery—are feeling the pressure to focus on improving their performance.

The questions are: Can it be done cheaper? Faster? Better? Performance-based management focuses heightened attention on these questions through the use of performance goals and measures. It has been said that what gets measured gets done.

Is this a fad? Maybe. There have been management improvement strategies before "performance management," and there will be others to come.

The real question for anyone managing a public enterprise (or any other sector) ought to be: What can I get done with the tools available to me? In this light, the question need not be what do I need to do for performance management but what can performance management do for me.

Recommended Responses

1. Performance-based management/measurement is all over the world in both the public and private sectors. Administrators of the public business, and especially the elected and appointed officials whose responsibility it is to lead that business, should acquire and maintain an awareness of emerging management trends, and be able to assess, choose, and apply those that will be of benefit to the U.S. government and economy.

2. A management initiative that emphasizes goals, measures of performance, and results can't be all bad; if nothing else, it is the law. It's

hard to see how this kind of focus, effectively led and managed, can do anything but help political leaders to accomplish their goals. A good starting point for incoming political leaders would be to get a copy of the Government Performance and Results Act itself, and keep it close at hand.

"GPRA Has Not Been Effective"

Are you sure?

What are your criteria? What could one reasonably expect?

The Bush administration which took office in 2001 judged GPRA not to have lived up to its potential.

The law could not officially be declared useless, however, because it seems so right (who can be against government programs having clear goals and measurable results?) that it would be hard to get rid of. And it provides the legal foundation for a set of core processes central to any management improvement initiative.

The policy seems to be to let the law run its course, and use it to the extent that it supports the President's Management Agenda.

There is nothing wrong with this approach. A given administration is not required to carry out all laws with enthusiasm.

But the judgment that GPRA has not been effective is premature.

The negative reaction to GPRA seems to have arisen largely as incoming political appointees looked at their agency's strategic plans, annual plans, and annual reports, and found them wanting. This is a little like coming upon someone who is in the middle of getting dressed, and saying he or she is not fully clothed.

GPRA requires learning. What is a strategic plan? How do you measure a program outcome? What kind of report will be effective? If the plans and reports looked bad in 2000, imagine what they looked like in 1996. The point is that an initiative such as GPRA cannot be implemented overnight. New skills have to be learned. New processes established.

What is the relationship of the work done under GPRA to the law itself? To the political appointees in charge?

Who or what is responsible?

Is it the law? Is it the career civil servants? Their political leaders? Both?

Recommended Responses
1. A little political art is needed. The practice of simply placing the previous administration on the floor and jumping up and down on its lifeless corpse is lacking in political art. It's a little too much. There are so many other ways to make a point if one needs to be made. A good rule of

thumb is: Don't make sweeping criticisms of the previous administration's activities without making a credible point in a credible way—with some facts and analysis.

2.   Make sure you have made a reasonable allowance for the time required for a given management reform to take effect. It is still too early to pass judgment on the Government Performance and Results Act. Any management initiative needs to be assessed in relation to a set of reasonable expectations. Much progress has been made to date. In particular, much learning has taken place and expertise gained in developing strategic plans, annual plans, and performance measures. Today the single most important remaining challenge is not the design and installation of goals and measures, but their use in improving decision making—and that responsibility rests squarely on the shoulders of political leaders.

"We Have Our Own System"

There are places in the government where some form of performance-based management has been used for some time.

It is not unusual to find some form of performance requirement in many types of programs—including direct and block grants, as well as credit, regulatory, and research activities. These requirements range from specific performance criteria to fairly unstructured performance reporting.

Some agency functions are more oriented toward performance measurement than others. Scientific, medical, and research programs are among them.

These agencies are data and methodology centric; they use information and measurement techniques all the time. Many were initially no more friendly to the performance measurement requirements of the Results Act than other agencies, but a few took the position that their existing performance information was sufficient to satisfy the requirements of the law.

GPRA calls for outcome measures. This is a pretty high standard.

But at least one large area of the government has stood out over the last 10 years for its insistence that:

- It already has a performance-based management system.
- The system has been in place for a long time.
- Everything is under control.

That agency is the Department of Defense (DoD).

The culture at DoD traces its performance-based management to the days of Robert McNamara and the "whiz kids."

But the press and others still report cost overruns, planes that don't fly, weapons that don't work, and strategies that are not effective.

It is hard to criticize the armed forces, the people who protect our country and way of life, our own sons and daughters who may be risking their lives.

But there is an attitude that is unique to the defense culture.

An example: A nationally known expert on performance measurement gave a presentation on the subject at a conference. His presentation impressed a representative of the Navy who asked that he come and make the same presentation to his boss, an admiral. At the appointed time and place, the presentation was made to the admiral, who sat at the end of a very long table with his senior staff sitting bolt upright on each side. At the end of the presentation, there was a long silence. The admiral then looked to the men on his left and then to the men on his right and said, "We've got this covered, haven't we?" At which point both flanks of the table came alive with concurring body language and "yes sirs." The admiral got up and left the room without acknowledging the presenter.

Recommended Responses
1. However unintended, there is an appearance of arrogance in some areas of the Department of Defense and the armed services. Those in the military ought to consciously be on guard against giving the appearance that they have everything under control. In a world increasingly at risk of terrorism, the ability of the military to protect the country may increasingly depend on humility, as there is a greater and greater need to leverage the active participation of the general population.
2. There is a widespread perception that while the Department of Defense may have a long tradition of performance management, its techniques are in need of updating. Incoming political appointees would do well to review whatever performance management system they find in their area of responsibility and come to their own conclusion about its comparability to what is happening in the private sector and in other areas of the government. If nothing else, the current emphasis on strategic planning and outcome measurement—which would include strategies for postwar rebuilding—needs to be more in evidence.

"It Doesn't Help Me"

This may very well be the case. Though it can sound like an offhand complaint, it can point to a very real problem.

Top-level political appointees are often dealing with issues that are not tied to the orderly world of performance-based management.

Performance-based management systems typically yield information on a predetermined schedule. The schedule may be monthly, quarterly, semi-annual, annual—whatever has been determined to be the best compromise between information availability and management needs.

Typically, when information is urgently needed, it is suffused by a political or management crisis. The time frame is now.

A story breaks on the evening news or in the morning papers. Phones ring at the White House and at cabinet agencies. How big is this problem? How many people does it affect? What are we doing to fix it? How much will it cost? How long will it take?

Much of the life of both senior political appointees and senior career executives involves dealing with such urgent issues.

Yet our information systems do not take them into account. By and large, the federal government does not have performance reporting systems for *now,* and not a lot of thought has been given to how that might be provided.

But these are legitimate needs, and any well-designed performance-based management system should take them into account.

Recommended Responses

1. Some proportion of the resources allocated to designing, installing, and using performance measurement systems should be reserved for ad hoc needs. A very small percentage—probably in the single digits—would probably be enough.
2. Top-level appointees should convene executives under them whose operations have ongoing performance management and measurement activities and systems to communicate their priorities and interests. Simply making these known would not only provide direction but stimulate engagement and perhaps even build momentum. There may not be a great deal that can be done in terms of tweaking the system to focus on new priorities. But the chances are that something can be done, and that would be a step in the right direction.

Designing Performance Indicators

Deciding on what performance indicators will be used to track program progress is often seen as a complicated and largely "methodological" activity, one that requires professional expertise in empirical and analytical techniques.

This may or may not be so.

Some program activities may require sophisticated techniques.

Many others do not.

Most should not.

The basic thrust of the Government Performance and Results Act was to help managers to manage, not to empower experts to analyze, evaluate, and ruminate.

Political appointees are the highest-level executives accountable to the American public for the management of public resources. Tracking performance is one of their most important responsibilities.

With or without the assistance of experts, appointees need to understand the issues, select the measures, and be able to explain the measures chosen—themselves.

Experts will almost never agree. All stakeholder views cannot be fully satisfied. Performance indicators can never tell the whole story by themselves. Resources almost always limit choices.

Top leaders need to step forward and accept full accountability.

"It's Not My Job to _____"

This kind of reaction can be found at all points in the performance management process, from design to use. It is taken up here because this stage in the process—the design stage—is pivotal to all that follows, and if there is one point in the process where political leadership and accountability is needed, it is at this stage.

This is because the emphasis in performance-based management almost everywhere, and especially in relation to the Government Performance and Results law, is on the measurement of progress toward outcomes. These are the intended results of the program, the services required by and provided to citizens.

The word *required* may seem strange and needs a word of explanation. It is not often used in contemporary discourse. It is used here to remind us that public services are not provided because they return a profit on investment, but because some element of the body politic supports them, wants them, needs them, or should have them.

So, delivering services—most of which are required by law—is one of the most important aspects of managing the government.

Since it is of great importance, political leaders should participate in and be accountable for the efficient and effective management of the programs through which those services are delivered.

Performance measures provide this accountability.

The better such measures are designed, the more likely it is that the desired performance will be achieved.

To be sure, the political process itself provides a substantial measure of accountability, as elections register voter approval and indicate priorities.

But performance measurement is where the rubber meets the road. What gets measured gets done—for the American people.

Recommended Responses

1. Politically appointed program managers should make it a point to acquire a basic understanding of performance measurement, including the design of performance measures. There is a language of performance measurement emerging all over the world that needs to be mastered and understood before it can be effectively applied. This would not be an arduous task. Reading one or two articles, a chapter in a book, or a Government Accountability Office (GAO) report would go a long way.

2. If there is one thing appointees should pay urgent attention to it is any information having to do with the performance of services they deliver to citizens. They should become masters of all major sources of information about their programs, from internal management information systems to external reports, articles, stories, and books.

"My Role Is Political"

This is a variant of the "It's Not My Job" reaction, but it is so prevalent and important as to merit separate consideration.

Sometimes it is deeply felt and deeply believed.

And it is often the case that it is accompanied by hard, long, and self-sacrificing work on behalf of the political agenda. One can admire the integrity of the position as well as the hard work.

But it is just plain wrong.

Political appointees are not just responsible for politics and policy. They are also responsible for management, and this includes processes and systems.

Management processes and systems require constant attention. Capital investments have to be made. Long-terms plans need to be developed and managed to conclusion. Many things having to do with management cannot be accomplished on a neat four-year (or 18-month) cycle, but if they are never started, they will never get done. Moreover, some level of responsibility needs to be accepted in regard to management initiatives initiated under previous administrations. This does not mean each administration must accept everything done by previous ones in relation to investments in management processes and systems; but it certainly does mean that it needs to be carefully considered within a context of responsibility that rises above a given political term.

The government, after all, serves all of us, all of the time.

Many political appointees come into government, serve their terms, and leave, without ever really accepting responsibility for the well-being of the management processes and systems under their control, or, perhaps more accurately, without accepting responsibility for more than the policy and political dimensions of their departments, programs, and functions.

They do not want to be seen as bad managers, and, for the most part, they are not. But neither would one say that they are notably good managers or exceptional managers. Looking back over a 30- or 40-year career, many career public servants can count on one hand the number of appointees who really rolled up their sleeves; mastered the details of a given management process, structure, or program; and took some risks to improve its management.

Recommended Responses
1. Political appointees need to see themselves as management executives as well as political and policy leaders. It's a whole new concept involving different skills and different work. It is often not as exciting as political and policy work. It does not often energize the ego. Much is done without recognition. But it is very important.
2. A good strategy would be to pick out one or two management areas for priority attention. These might be areas of special expertise or interest. Focusing on a small number would help to assure that something gets done. Let it be known that these are the things you are interested in. Let it be known that you see this as your "long term" contribution to the institution of government, not related to party politics and policies. And then ask for help. You'll probably be pleasantly surprised by the enthusiastic response from career professionals.

"Our Stuff Is Really Tough"

In practice, this remark, made by a senior political appointee, is delivered a little more artfully than it used to be.

In the early stages of GPRA implementation, the statement would simply have been, "You can't really measure our programs." Everyone was struggling with initial attempts at measurement, and this was a fairly routine response.

Today, the full statement would more likely be, "Well, of course, we do have measures for our GPRA plans and reports, and we track things pretty closely for the President's Management Agenda, but, you know, it's really hard to measure what we do."

So there has been some progress. But the notable aspect of both responses is the distance they imply between the political appointee and his or her agency's performance measurement activity. Measurement is something that happens over there, in the GPRA and PMA areas. Measurement is "pretty complicated."

Performance measurement as a priority activity worthy of the personal attention of a department or agency head, as something that is essential to good management and good public administration, is less in evidence.

If it were more in evidence, we would have more of a sense from senior political leaders that they are genuinely engaged in coming to grips with challenging measurement issues. We would feel engagement and commitment. We would hear something like this:

> You can't really measure many programs, and I'm not sure measurement is the issue so much as management. GPRA was intended to improve the quality of service delivery. We don't have the resources—no one does—to design and use perfect "measures." Perfect measures would be very expensive, and there has been no separate appropriation for GPRA, so we have to do the best we can with what we have. But working with what we had, we chose these measures, for these reasons, and we are open to suggestions as to how we can improve them.

Recommended Responses

1. Senior leaders should be fully engaged in the process of designing and using the performance measures for their most important programs. They owe the public no less. Performance measurement is in the first instance a leadership activity. And in the second instance it is an accountability function. Both rest squarely on the shoulders of agency leaders.
2. Not only should leaders understand the issues related to the measurement of their own programs, but they should have a working understanding of the measurement of similar and related programs in other agencies and in other countries. If the United States is to enjoy a position of leadership in today's world, how can that be done without an awareness of how similar activities are managed elsewhere.

"It's Hard to Measure Research"

The history of this issue over the last 10 years is fascinating, and illustrative of continuing confusion in some aspects of performance-based management.

Early on, there was a strong feeling among some GPRA framers that research should perhaps be treated differently from other activities.

Paralleling this was the related thought that GPRA was intended to help managers to manage, rather than measurers to measure.

Had the two thoughts come together, it would have been recognized that the issue was not how to measure research but how to manage it.

And recall that the word *measure* crept into usage in place of the intended word *indicators*.

While the thought of managing research is still very uncomfortable for researchers, it is less uncomfortable than the thought of measuring it.

And, in the years since, the sense that even the most challenging activities, such as research, can benefit from the application of GPRA requirements has grown in acceptance.

From this perspective, some sense of strategy (as in strategic plans), some sense of planned annual activities (as in annual plans), and some type of annual reporting against intended goals (as in annual reports that include information on progress toward outcome measures) are appropriate.

During this same period, echoes of this issue could be heard on the Hill, where some thought that research programs should be more closely monitored. Agencies as diverse as the National Science Foundation and the Smithsonian Institution have come under congressional scrutiny in relation to their selection (read *performance*) criteria for awarding grants.

From this perspective, the research community needs to acknowledge that a scientist with a grant is a citizen to whom the resources of other citizens have been assigned for responsible pursuit of research activities in the national interest, whether basic or applied.

The peer review process is not sufficient to satisfy this responsibility, because it is a closed community wherein a closed group of citizens with a vested interest in a very specialized activity talk to themselves.

In short, scientists of all types have a responsibility to give some thought to how they communicate what they are doing to their fellow citizens. Truly impressive and pioneering research is at increasing risk because the scientists doing it are not communicating the value of their activities.

It may be that GPRA requirements for a strategic plan, annual plan, and annual report focusing on outcomes may have to be seen in the light of the research context. But the research community needs to make a credible effort at communicating what it is doing.

The issue, more so with research than many other areas, is not so much measurement or even management as it is communication.

Recommended Responses

1. Basic research: The spirit, if not the letter, of GPRA is appropriate, and it is growing more and more necessary in today's legislative and management environment. Rarely do those engaged in basic research simply show up in their laboratories and throw chemicals together to see what happens. They start with questions, hunches, and unexplainable processes. There is no reason why these cannot be recorded in terms of what is to be addressed, what actually takes place, and next steps based on findings. Individual researchers should maintain a simple log explaining what they are going to do, why, and what the result is.

2. Applied research: The recommendation above applies with added responsibility. And an effort should be made to collect information about the effect of the application. Sometimes this will be available in

statistical form. At other times, it will be available only in the form of stories about exceptional effects. Both are valuable and can be starting points. Clearly, direct cause-and-effect attribution cannot be definitively established without experimental and control groups, which would be expensive and take too long. But such statistics and stories as can be gathered would be a good start.

"People Don't Agree"

Truer words were never spoken, but that's one of the major issues performance-based management is meant to address.

Interestingly, this viewpoint used to be expressed a little differently several years ago. Then the comment most often heard was, "It's hard to get people to agree."

There's a difference of considerable importance. The earlier comment implies that some effort at trying to get people to agree is important. The current one is a kind of throwing up of the hands without much interest or effort.

In truth, there never really has been much effort to obtain and consider stakeholder views. But there have been some efforts and some good examples that opened the door to good things. The Veterans Benefits Administration did a survey of stakeholders that turned up some pretty frank feelings, and the resulting dialogue was considered beneficial for all concerned.

It is true that people don't agree. Congress has a point of view. The Office of Management and Budget (OMB) has a point of view. Interest groups, academic institutions, and stakeholders all have different points of view.

Each one of these points of view might be splintered into a number of additional views depending on the purpose for which measures are being designed.

There is nothing wrong with different points of view. This is normal and to be expected.

The whole purpose of stakeholder involvement is to reach some kind of understanding on the purposes and measures that are appropriate. It is *not* likely that complete agreement will be reached. It *is* likely that there will be some disagreement.

But failure to open a line of communication to stakeholders is not only poor politics but bad management and bad public service.

As public servants, elected and appointed officials in particular have a special responsibility to seek and take into account the views of citizens, in or out of the government.

Recommended Responses

1. Often stakeholder comments are not widely sought because of time and cost factors. The plan or report has to be done now. There is no money. But there are ways to open the door even in challenging circumstances. The best (but most expensive and time-consuming) method would be to have meetings with stakeholder groups. Alternatively (if a modest amount of time and money are available), a survey could be designed and mailed out, which could be followed with in-depth interviews to illustrate major points of view. A variant of this would be a letter sent to major stakeholders simply asking for their views (as opposed to a survey containing a number of specific questions). And (if there is almost no time and money), a notice could be posted on the web asking for comments.

2. If there is no time, no money, and no possibility of seeking stakeholder input, the resulting product should be distributed broadly, explaining these circumstances and inviting comment on a retrospective basis. If this approach is taken, the invitation to comment should include a succinct statement of why the included measures were selected so that respondents can review the thought process as well as the specific measure.

"It's All Too Technical"

Well, if that's the way it looks to you, then you and your agency are on the wrong track.

This is not rocket science.

The Results Act was intended to help you manage government programs and report results to citizens.

If it does not do that, then there is something wrong with the way it is being implemented in your agency.

Emphatically, GPRA is not technical. It does not require technicians, scholars, consultants, or other sophisticated skills. Common sense—starting where you are, using what you have—would be a good effort. What makes sense to you? What do you think would make sense for the public?

Strategic plans can be as basic as: Where are you starting from? Where do you see your agency going? What do you have to do to get there? What don't you have? And how are you going to get what you need?

This is management 101. Many agency strategic plans do not even incorporate all of these basic elements. Almost all are missing some. There is no one-size-fits-all template or score sheet.

To give no thought to strategic issues during your tenure as an appointed public servant would be to ignore a pretty fundamental responsibility.

And the same goes for outcome measures. If it does not help you and your agency to communicate what you are doing to stakeholders—and especially to citizens—something is awry.

Remember, the basic purpose of a measure under GPRA is to report progress toward intended results, whatever it is that has been promised to citizens.

If the strategic plans and performance measures that come across your desk seem "technical," that should be a warning sign to you that your staff is off track.

They may have good reasons for proposing a measure that to you seems technical or not helpful in terms of your ability to manage or report. But those good reasons need to be assessed in relation to your practical sense of what will do the job.

Recommended Responses
1. It is always wise to get some feedback from key stakeholders. The more the better. If there are political reasons why you cannot do this in a broad public way, then at least consider some one-on-one meetings or phone calls to key individuals and groups.
2. Send the proposal (strategic plan, annual plan, annual report, or outcome measure) to citizens in your hometown and get feedback from your department's constituents. Set up a small focus group. Go to a neighborhood or organization.

"No One Really Cares"

This comment is made in many forms. "Congress doesn't care." "My managers don't care." Sometimes even: "OMB doesn't care" (in spite of the President's Management Agenda and the Program Assessment Rating Tool, or PART, process).

And the most potentially important of all: "The public doesn't care."

You know, there's only one way to answer these comments that suits the issue: So what?

This is one of those issues that is so important, so much a part of public service and being a public servant, that it ought to go to the top of your priority list no matter who says what.

The fact is that you do not *have* a job; it isn't yours. You've been given a trust. You do not *have* a budget; it isn't yours. You've been given it in trust.

You are a servant of the public—whether you are a Republican or a Democrat.

You hold the resources of citizens in trust to carry out the work they have assigned to you.

Sometimes it is useful to recall what individual citizens and taxpayers look like. They include executives and managers, plumbers and electricians, laborers and unskilled workers; the rich and the poor; mothers and fathers, uncles and aunts.

It would be a good thing if every time the government spent or managed a dollar, the face of a citizen appeared instead of George Washington.

Performance-based management is simple, fundamental, and familiar. All of us have some kind of family budget, or the idea of one in our heads. We have certain things we want to accomplish. And we track progress toward our goals with great interest.

That is all this is.

There may be numbers, terms, requirements, plans, and reports. But that is just the system of the United States government. That's the way things work in Washington.

If you don't like the requirements for GPRA, the PMA, and PART, don't ignore the worthwhile purpose they serve.

It is your most fundamental responsibility.

Recommended Responses

1. All political leaders, and especially those in significant leadership positions, should proactively support and advance the concept of performance in government management and service delivery. If there is some lack of attention, enthusiasm, or acceptance, then apply the same political art that got your party elected. Politics and management at the leadership level is in some part an art form. Be persuasive. Attract people to the cause. Build a coalition. Develop common ground for different points of view. Pay at least as much attention to getting performance management effectively established in your agency as you did to getting your party elected or being appointed to your present position.

2. Try to go out and see some of the programs and organizations where performance-based management is working well in the public and private sectors. When you see how good it can be when it is done well, how great are the benefits in terms of improved service and reduced costs, your enthusiasm will get the best of you, and you'll go at it with renewed energy. Try it and see.

"My Deputy (Secretary) Does That"

The surest way of not accomplishing your top priorities is to entrust them to someone else, no matter how competent, loyal, or highly placed that person is.

That's true everywhere in life, and it's true in Washington.

But many do just that. Secretaries assign the "management" of their department to deputy secretaries while they handle the "political side."

Speeches, appearances on radio and TV, answering phone calls and letters, and going to important social events jam the schedules of top political leaders.

It's seductive. You're important. Your agency is responsible for thousands of employees, millions of people, and billions of dollars.

There is only one person who will take your top priorities as seriously as you do, and who will be as effective in carrying them out—and that is you.

The only question, then, is whether setting performance goals, designing performance measures, and managing toward performance results is important to you.

How can they not be.

You must have a short list of top priorities. And you must work systematically toward them, no matter how many other demands there are from other sources.

It has been said that what gets measured gets done.

Measures can help you. Put them where you want to go. Refer to them. Check progress against them. Ask for help to achieve them. Let it be known that they are your priorities.

Your leadership position vests you with the ability to set priorities and to have them paid attention to by your staff.

This advice is passed along from former to new political appointees repeatedly: You can come to Washington, show up at the office every day, stay out of trouble, go to social events, and leave a good fellow. Or you can come to Washington and use your position to accomplish things. And if you try to get things done, you will find that you will have to fight to keep your priorities on the table.

Performance goals and measures are a way to keep your priorities at the top of everyone else's list.

Recommended Responses

1. Don't assign away to someone else all of the responsibility for day-to-day management. Reserve the most important issues for yourself, using your deputy as your assistant. Clearly state your top priorities, and develop specific goals and measures for each. Overlay these goals across your existing management structures and processes.

2. You can give your priorities an enormous boost by walking around and talking to the people who are working on them. Have someone draw up a chart that shows all the people working on each of your priorities. Include everyone from the lowest clerk to the highest executive. Reserve 30 minutes three times a week to walk into the office of one of these

people completely unannounced. Pick an office worker one week, an executive the next. Make it person to person, not political appointee to staff. Make human contact. Follow up with a note. Mention what is being discussed at your executive staff meetings. Express appreciation. You'll be amazed at the effect on morale and productivity.

"The PART Is Not about Measures ..."

"it's about results"—goes this odd but not uncommon remark.

To those who have followed the evolution of performance-based management in the federal government, this remark seems to come from left field; nevertheless, it is being made.

And, more importantly, it is sometimes part of a broader attitude that relates measures to the Government Performance and Results Act and then relates GPRA to the previous administration—as distinguished from the President's Management Agenda, which is this administration's approach ... sometimes leaving the question unanswered as to whether measures are or are not part of the PMA.

And, if that paragraph is hard to follow, it accurately conveys some contemporary thinking at very high political levels.

It is easy to make the situation clear.

The Government Performance and Results Act is a law and requires performance measures.

GPRA is the legal foundation for much of the PMA.

The Program Assessment Rating Tool, or PART, uses the budget process to drive performance metrics through all kinds of management systems, levels of government, and types of programs.

The President's Management Agenda, through the PART, focuses squarely on results, specifically looks for measures, emphasizes the need for data and analysis to confirm them, and provides examples. Succinct OMB commentary on each of these elements may be found in the Performance and Management Assessments, which are used to summarize the PART analysis for each program.

In fact, a close look at the PART requirements might lead to this conclusion: The guidelines press hard against existing law, regulation, and practice in the pressure that they place on grantees and subgrantees not under direct federal authority to accept a fair share of accountability for performance where federal dollars are involved.

In general, the word *measurement* is less in use today than earlier, being to a substantial extent subsumed under the word *results*. But the pressure is far stronger today than earlier to have data, analysis, and program evaluation studies to track performance.

Recommended Responses
1. Agency leaders should read through the PART instructions and guidelines. They are stunningly focused on program management, results, and the quality of information available to document both. They are not theoretical or overly focused on analytical methodology. But they are seriously and intensely focused on management, results, and information.
2. Leaders should also read half a dozen of the PART analyses. They are not long. They are well formatted and very clear. They ask for fundamental information—the kind of information every citizen should have and every public administrator should provide for every government program.

Aligning Management Processes

Effective management starts with accountability; accountability starts with alignment; alignment means clear lines of responsibility coordinated to achieve specific objectives.

It seems so clear.

So simple.

But many new political appointees find management processes that are anything but "aligned."

They are "shocked," "appalled," "confused," and "dumbfounded" by "the mess" in Washington.

Well, it's true. It isn't perfect. It's very imperfect.

Congress passes laws and assigns them to agencies. Agencies grow by accretion. It's not necessarily a rational process.

But performance-based management can help, and in fact is ideally suited to help in this context.

GPRA requires goals and measures of performance, which, in turn, can be used to establish clear lines of accountability without requiring a "reorganization" of structures, processes, or accounts. This may lead to or be accompanied by a reorganization, but it does not require it.

This can be an enormous benefit to appointees. With an average tenure of 18 months, a political appointee who decides on a reorganization may not be around to see it through.

"This Organization Is a Mess"

If you think your organization is a mess, that your bureaus, divisions, offices, and branches seem not to reflect an ordered intelligence, you are experiencing one of the most common reactions among incoming political leaders who have no previous Washington experience.

The organizational structure of many agencies often presents a jumbled, sometimes haphazard appearance.

You will do yourself, your organization, and your party a favor by not blaming the people who work in those units and by not assuming that "they" have deliberately cluttered the landscape for their own malevolent purposes.

Departments, bureaus, agencies, and organizational units do not emerge whole from some scientifically pure design process.

They are created piecemeal over long periods of time as the congressional and executive branches of government set and reset their respective priorities. Overlay the changing interplay of these tension-filled forces with the constant coming and going of political parties and the melding, unmelding, and remelding of the relationships between senior career civil servants and senior political appointees, and the outcome may seem more understandable.

Nor is "reorganization" a likely solution, at least not in the short term—and that is all many political leaders have.

The time and energy likely to be lost in connection with a reorganization should be carefully weighed against the likely benefits. This does not mean that processes and structures should not be redesigned, but large-scale reorganizations should be approached with caution.

The assumption of new duties and responsibilities takes time. You will need to work out relationships with a new group of managers. If moving people to new duties reflects the same patterns as hiring people for new duties, many of those placed in new positions will not work out as hoped, perhaps as many as 50 percent.

And, in the meantime, you have scared the creativity and risk-taking impetus right out of the organization—the very qualities you need for top-level performance.

Recommended Responses
1. Performance-based management, carefully focused around a small set of priority goals and measures, can be an effective strategy. Use performance-based goals and measures to overlay a fuzzy organization with a sharp focus.
2. Establish teams made up of units, parts of units, and individuals in the way that you feel offers the best chance to achieve your goals. Leave the existing structure alone. Hold regular team meetings and allow all top executives and as many non-executives as possible to attend. This will partially satisfy those who may be offended by the fact that their subordinates are on the team while they are not.

3. Put in place some kind of incentive structure that rewards team performance.

"Our Account Structure Doesn't Work"

Unfortunately, this is true in many agencies, and it is by no means a perception held only by political leaders. Career public servants and almost anyone else knowledgeable about the federal government has a similar view.

In many agencies, the account structure is impenetrable. In some agencies today, there are chief financial officers and budget office directors who will tell you in an informal moment that they really don't know what is happening with the flow of dollars through their accounts except in the most general way.

Here are some of the remarks heard on this issue:
*   All I know is that's about what they get every year.
*   I don't exactly know what happens with that money.
*   That's a deal we have with the Appropriations Committee.
*   The ranking member insists on funding that.
*   That office never responds to the budget [office's] call.
*   I had to guess at that; we have no idea what the runout costs are.

CFOs and senior budget officers can be pretty lonely jobs. They often live in the middle of a chaos that would not stand close scrutiny, and they know it.

But it's hardly their fault.

Agency account structures reflect the same ebb and flow of politics and policies as do agency organizational structures. The two—structures and accounts—are often closely linked. Congress passes a law. An agency creates an organizational unit and an account line. A new cabinet secretary has a priority and creates a new subunit with a new sub-account line.

Organizations and accounts once created are hard to separate, revise, or abolish. If you are the manager of a unit with an account, whether it's rational or not, it's hard to say it doesn't make sense. It's your job.

From the standpoint of performance-based management, however, a messy account structure cannot simply be walked away from. Knowing the costs of goods and services delivered to the public is important, especially since as public servants—political or career—we manage public funds in trust, on behalf of our fellow citizens.

It is incumbent upon political leaders to take some positive steps to improve financial accounting and the attribution of costs.

Recommended Responses
1. For the short term, some steps should be taken to rationalize financial planning and cost attribution. This may well involve preparing an over-

lay to the existing budget that seeks to rationalize the structure and uses informed best estimates as a temporary measure. There is nothing wrong with estimates as long as the process for generating them is exposed to full public view. Do something and tell how you did it.

2. For the longer term, some steps should be taken to develop a better account structure. Given the fact that any structure will inevitably be superseded by unfolding events, it will probably be wise to develop a data-based system that has the flexibility to change. At some point, OMB will probably have to develop an overarching structure based on a generic list of core public services with uniform accounting practices for each.

"Performance Budgeting Is a Dream"

This statement, made in an unguarded moment by a high-ranking political appointee, is an extreme expression of a very widely held feeling.

It is made more significant by the fact that the person who said it is a veteran appointee, having served in several administrations, and is experienced in budget operations.

Given the widely acknowledged "messiness" of organizational and accounting structures in the government and the widely understood reasons for them, serious expectations that performance-based budgeting will ever be a reality are rare, despite mantras and scorecards to the contrary.

Putting aside for the moment some of the obviously not helpful feelings and inclinations this kind of remark suggests—including discouragement, cynicism, narrow vision, and lack of commitment to the future of government—there remains a more serious problem.

There is a widespread perception that performance budgeting is only or predominantly an accounting issue.

Starting from this perspective, the road ahead is long and daunting. Federal account structures are a mess. They will take time to fix. Agencies cannot fix their structures unless the government itself (OMB) changes its accounts. Eventually, Congress will have to buy in.

But it is the right way to go, and everyone else is going there, all over the world in the public and private sectors. If we cannot efficiently and effectively align and attribute costs, we will not only waste public resources but also be unable to transact business.

Steps have to be taken now toward the long-term goal of account restructuring. Some agencies have taken giant steps toward account redesign and activity-based costing. Many others have done much less.

Often overlooked is an enormous present, real-time opportunity. Before performance budgeting is an accounting issue, it is an attitude, a mind-set, and a process.

We can talk and think about performance budgeting now. In many ways the dialogue is the substance of the intended goal. Having aligned accounts is an important but not necessary element of performance budgeting. Aligned account structures will make performance budgeting easier; their absence does not prevent it.

Robust, engaged, dynamic, intense dialogue at every level within federal agencies about the relationship between costs and results would be a magnificent outcome. That dialogue alone would be a great achievement.

There are many ways to discuss costs without having a perfect account system. Costs can be estimated, extrapolated, benchmarked, hypothesized, and modeled.

Former OMB Director Mitch Daniels captured the essence of what is needed when he called for a "spirited dialogue" about costs and results. We owe American citizens no less.

Recommended Responses

1. In addition to taking thoughtful and necessary steps toward eventual account restructuring, agency leaders should develop a specific capacity to estimate costs relative to results—in the absence of account alignment. They and their staffs should become experts in the techniques of estimation. They should know them, use them, and be able to defend them. There will be no perfect answers, but there ought to be well-considered ones.
2. Leaders should explicitly encourage dialogue about costs and results in their agencies. Leaders can create incentives by talking about performance budgeting, asking for ideas, expressing interest in those who are moving ahead. Forums might be established by program area or goal with the specific purpose of seeking new ways of thinking and encouraging the development of new ideas and methods.

"The PART Process Is a Pain"

That may be true. But if it is, it's the kind of pain you should have more of.

The Program Assessment Rating Tool (PART) process is so right headed, so well intended, so reasonably conceived and managed, and so utterly in keeping with the spirit of public service, that it ought to be at the top of your priority, painful or not.

As OMB's latest and most advanced effort to support performance-based, results-oriented government, the PART has the potential for making a major positive contribution to improve government performance.

In the past, the budget process was a black box. The public, Congress, and even agencies knew little about how and why decisions were made. For the most part, only an agency's senior budget officer and a few very high-level political appointees really knew what transpired in the deliberations with OMB. Such information was closely held in no small part because it was something of a status symbol to be "in the know." For the agency's budget officer, who is normally a career civil servant, such information was a source of power and influence throughout the agency. Get on the wrong side of the senior budget officer, and you might not get a piece of information with important implications for your program.

What happened within OMB was also obscure. An agency might know how its own funding decisions were made, but it knew very little about the decisions relative to other agencies or about the process as a whole. The decision-making process within OMB lacked systematic structure, allowing significant variation from one budget officer to another.

The goal of the PART process is to provide a standard, structured, empirically based, public format for making budget decisions. Everyone can see what the process is. Everyone can judge whether OMB has made good decisions. All of this information is available to citizens.

Throughout the process of developing and implementing the PART, OMB has shown an unprecedented willingness to subject its thinking to wide and expert review. By and large, its decisions have been transparently motivated by a strong focus on effective, information-informed management, focused on results.

This is one pain all political leaders should bear without complaint. It's too important.

Recommended Responses

1. The PART process is the ultimate management alignment tool. Focused as it is on the connection between program objectives, goals, measures, and the management processes that link them, the PART can be a powerful lever for improved government performance. Rather than seeing the PART as another "paper exercise," agency leaders should actively use it to achieve worthwhile ends.

2. In particular, agency leaders should take a proactive approach to the entire PART process. OMB has said it will do PART reviews on 20 percent of the federal inventory each year for five years. Rather than wait for the PART process to come to them, agency leaders should take the process to OMB. This would give them the maximum amount of time to consider program design and management improvements in the public interest.

"There's So Much Duplication and Overlap"

That's true and not a bad starting point for a discussion of performance alignment, as long as you realize that duplication and overlap result from issues that are systemic and are not caused by incompetent bureaucrats who don't know how to manage programs.

Our governmental system is not designed to produce perfectly designed programs; it is designed to fairly represent the many and varied views of citizens. Through the process of counting votes, whether in municipal elections or in congressional deliberations, dissimilar interests are pushed and pulled into a semblance of agreement.

That imperfect product is then shipped off to an agency for implementation. Many decisions have to be made to get the process going. The political process often complicates an already challenging management—read *alignment*—issue. A cabinet secretary urgently wants to get the new money out to constituents, perhaps before a management information system can be designed. Maybe even before the content of the program is fully known.

There is nothing wrong with this system. It is the American political system at work.

Neither is it a reason to forgo honest effort at applying the principles of performance-based management.

If there are overlapping and duplicative programs and parts of programs, then common sense demands that as the representatives of your fellow citizens now on watch—now in a position to see, understand, and remedy some of the unintended consequences of previous political processes—you take some affirmative steps toward improvement.

If someone else had your job in Washington, would you want them to throw up their hands and say, "This is a mess," or would you want them to make an effort to make it better?

Whatever you do will take courage and persistence. Programs are tied to money and no one wants to give up dollars. Those getting the dollars don't want to lose what they buy and those managing the programs that dispense them don't want to lose their jobs. Members of Congress will not be quiet. Businesspeople, as well as political and civic leaders, will express strong views. Resistance will be strong everywhere.

Recommended Responses
1. The most important strategic thing you can do to handle the challenge of overlapping and duplicative programs is to take the high road. No one can truly be against improving the effectiveness of public resources. Everyone will instantly resist an approach that looks to be entirely political, or that lacks careful thought and reliable data. Using sloppy

language, letting irritation suggest condemnation, or indirectly pointing the finger at civil servants will not help.

2. Take some steps both within and outside your agency. Start in your own agency. Map out related programs. Meet with program directors. Understand clearly what each similar program does. Be able to explain how they relate to each other. Give each program the benefit of the doubt. Then add them up, and estimate results and costs on a comparative basis. Take some positive steps toward streamlining or consolidating. In regard to similar programs in other agencies, reach out to those agency leaders and see if you can begin a dialogue. You can't control whether your offer is accepted, but you can make the offer.

"We Have No Control Over That"

There is a line of thinking to the effect that if a program does not have a specific legislative requirement for performance measures, then there is no federal responsibility to track performance.

According to this view, many federal programs that channel funds to state and local governments through such mechanisms as revenue sharing, block grants, formula grants, and competitive grants—which do not have specific legislative requirements—were established with the specific purpose of providing maximum flexibility to recipients. Any encroachment on this flexibility is seen as being fundamentally at odds with the intent of the initial program design.

And, even if it is necessary or desirable to track performance in such programs, how can it be done when there are no specific requirements?

The first thing that can be said about this kind of thinking is that in today's world it seems both very conservative and very dated.

Twenty years ago, few would have disagreed. A formula grant program meant hands off from Washington. Most such programs had minimal reporting requirements.

Today, there is a growing sense that all programs need to have a performance dimension, even those that do not have specific legislative requirements for monitoring performance, as well as those that specifically prohibit federal data collection requirements.

This does not mean that the federal government can impose performance reporting where it is not legislatively authorized.

But it seems to mean almost anything else.

OMB's Program Assessment Rating Tool includes a number of requirements that press for performance information. For example, in relation to formula, block, and competitive grant programs, it asks: "Does the program collect grantee performance data on an annual basis and make it available to the public in a transparent and meaningful manner?"

A recent notice from the Department of Housing and Urban Development to recipients of Community Development Block Grant funds provides detailed guidance on how to gather performance information, asks grantees to submit a plan for collecting performance data, and asks those grantees that are not collecting such data to explain why.

Clearly, grantees are not being "required" to have and use performance information, but just as clearly they are being asked to take proactive steps.

There seems to be a growing sense that the receipt of public dollars brings some fundamental aspects of accountability. A block, formula, or other grant program does not mean an exemption from the responsibility to spend dollars wisely. The funds do not "belong" to grantees as a matter of "right."

Recommended Responses
1. There are many ways to develop performance information, even where there are no specific legislative requirements. Pick out a program or activity and encourage the development of informal partnerships. Set up meetings and forums for discussion and information sharing. In the best circumstance, federal, state, and local grantees can work together without a specific legislative requirement. Some of this is already happening. State and local governments, seeing the increasing interest in performance management, are pressing upward toward their federal partners, and the federal government is pressing downward. These inclinations can be encouraged by all parties through joint ventures that may begin as nothing more than information sharing but that may mature into joint design and use of performance information.
2. If state and local governments show no interest in direct collaboration with the federal government, the collection and dissemination of good practices can be a very effective way to take an initial non-threatening step and jump-start a dialogue.

"We Can't Cost Things Out"

A large part of any effort to align management structures and processes to achieve the highest level of performance has to do with cost attribution.

In general, three things need to happen to lay the foundation for an effective performance system. First, the elements of an activity need to be identified, grouped, and sequenced. Second, an accountability system needs to be superimposed over the sequence. And, third, each element in the sequence needs to be costed out.

Each of these steps brings its own challenges; none is easy. All of them involve imposing a performance logic chain over existing structures, processes, and customs. If organizational structures and processes are imperfectly aligned, having been created piecemeal as a result of legislative and political currents, they are at the same time entrenched and subject to enormous inertia.

In no area is this more apparent than in regard to the attribution of resources. Few owners of a structure, process, or budget will easily yield parts of their kingdoms to another kingdom, especially one as apparently ephemeral and mysterious as "performance management."

Put simply, no one wants to give up control of his or her budget.

But something on this order has to happen as the government moves toward a performance-based management system.

And it can be done.

The starting point is estimation.

If present accounting processes and structures do not provide cost information to support performance-oriented management, then the only starting point is estimation.

To do nothing, or to wait until account structures are redesigned while public dollars are flowing through the system with no one making any effort at gauging the flow, is not acceptable. Individuals would not do that with their own money; it shouldn't be done in government with other people's money.

Holding in mind the thought that the money you dispense and manage is not yours helps to fuel resolve and encourage action.

Recommended Responses

1. When you don't have all the data you need, estimate. Cost attribution is an essential aspect of performance-based management and a fundamental responsibility for the management of public resources. To do nothing because present accounting systems and structures are out of alignment or worse is to walk away from a public trust. Some effort at estimation needs to be made. There is likely no one right estimation method. Experts can be called in to help with technical issues. But it is likely that judgment calls will have to be made. As long as the method is documented so that others can see it and comment, a basic responsibility has been met. It is possible that feedback in relation to whatever is done will substantially improve the process.

2. Whatever cost-estimation method is used, a useful second step would be to compare the results to similar processes in and out of the government. These comparisons will be rough but may yield helpful information. They will certainly continue the process of learning about cost estimation and attribution.

"Our Data Systems Don't Match Up"

Often agency data systems are only slightly less disjointed than agency account structures.

And for many of the same reasons.

An issue arises and gathers extensive press coverage. Congress responds by creating a new program and presses for rapid implementation. Citizens and interest groups beat the drums. The incumbent administration finds itself in the glare of daily news coverage. The agency head gets a call from the Office of the President: "Just get it done; the press coverage has got to stop." Agency political leaders make it clear to their staff that money has got to hit the street pronto.

There is nothing wrong with this scenario. It is the American political system at work. The people speak and the government acts.

But there is something lost on the management side. Inside the agency, career public servants will have pointed out that there is a need for a management information system. Without it, they will argue, it will be difficult to manage the program properly. Any significant management problem that may arise will have the potential for becoming a political problem, because without proper management controls—including a good data system—the agency will be unable to document and analyze what is happening. It will look incompetent because it cannot describe the problem accurately.

In the heat of the moment, data is not a priority.

Sometimes there is enough time to design and implement an information system. But rarely will it be consistent with other existing systems, each of which was implemented under similar urgent conditions.

Sometimes the information systems implemented during one administration in one agency will be coordinated if the senior political executives have an interest in the issue. But rarely are they coordinated across administrations.

Information systems, like budget account structures, grow through accretion. They often reflect a patchwork of political emergencies and priorities.

They may be written in different computer languages, contain disparate data elements, and operate under varying protocols. Rarely is there a way to conveniently gather and analyze information across similar or related programs.

Eventually, government-wide standards will be necessary to support effective performance-based management.

Recommended Responses

1. As is the case in relation to rationalizing budget account structures, agency leaders need to accept some measure of responsibility for the long term. It will take years to standardize existing management information systems. But some steps can and should be taken toward this

long-term task. Commissioning a study of the existing systems and preparing alternative courses of action would be one starting point.

2. Something needs to be done in the short term as well. One approach would be to identify a short list of priority programs based on such criteria as importance and dollar amount. Then, using this short list, design a statistically significant sample of program beneficiaries for each. Based on this sample, standardize core data elements and extrapolate back to the universe. The results may not be useful for making individual decisions regarding benefits, but they can at least inform broad-scale management and policy decisions.

"There's No Accountability System"

It is an often-voiced lament among political appointees that they have no means for holding career civil servants accountable.

The lament continues: "Career civil servants are so hard to discipline and/or remove that it is not worth the trouble. Senior career civil servants are closely allied with congressional committees and private interest groups who will cause trouble on their behalf." And so on.

In fact, it is probably easier to discipline or remove a senior career civil servant in the government than it is to take the same steps in regard to an employee of a large private sector firm. (Note: The same cannot be said for less senior civil servants, who operate under a different tenure system.) Each sector has procedures to assure fair and orderly processing and adjudication.

And the highest-level career civil servants, those who are in the Senior Executive Service (SES), have no real tenure at all. When the SES was created, senior executives who opted to join the new system gave up a good deal of the protection they had enjoyed under the previous system in return, it was projected, for greater opportunities for career flexibility, advancement, and executive bonuses.

If there is a need to remove an SES executive, all that needs to be done is to offer a reassignment to some barren outpost, the least attractive field or operational unit in the system. If the offer is declined, the executive has no job. If it is accepted, he or she is out of the way.

This may sound brutal, but it is true.

The real reason that political leaders often do not take such steps is that they are not willing to take on the task. One can hardly blame them. It is not pleasant. Anyone who has ever managed an organization of any size understands that there are times when it has to be done.

But the ultimate step is not the only one available. Leaders have many accountability levers that are rarely used. Annual evaluation ratings, bonuses, and incentive systems can be very effective—if seriously applied.

And there are a whole host of such levers that are far more subtle, such as shining the sun on those who are going in the right direction and raining on others.

This is not rocket science.

To someone with some management experience in the public sector, the "I can't hold them accountable" lament is the sure sign of an amateur.

Recommended Responses

1. Unpleasant though it may be, political leaders should thoroughly acquaint themselves with the legal procedures for disciplining and removing an employee. There are some basic steps that must be followed. They are neither many nor difficult, but they are essential—such as making written notations on a calendar or other format to document unacceptable performance.

2. There are many ways to establish accountability prior to taking disciplinary action. Incoming appointees should very soon develop a specific strategy for establishing accountability. Many come to Washington and leave without ever coming to grips with this issue. They seem to expect that since they are in the leadership role, others will carry out orders. It may be necessary to take specific disciplinary steps in at least one specific case to demonstrate your seriousness. Whatever the strategy, it should include a clear understanding of the process for disciplining or removing a persistently uncooperative or incompetent individual. In particular, disciplinary processes usually require some written record to support the action. If this is known in advance, it is very easy to make notations on an appointments calendar. If this is known and understood in advance, it is very easy to do; if it is not known, it can never be fixed.

Using Performance Information

An often-heard statement about performance information is that it is not actually used, that its primary utility is to fulfill the paperwork requirements of the Government Performance and Results Act.

Normally, those making this statement are outside observers. They are GAO analysts, OMB budget examiners, congressional staffers, or outside experts and observers.

We may take this as one order of magnitude on the GPRA implementation scale.

But when this kind of sentiment is expressed by a high-ranking political appointee, we have moved several orders of magnitude in the wrong direction.

Why?

Because if it is said by a cabinet secretary, deputy secretary, assistant secretary, or other high-ranking political leader, it is a de facto policy statement.

It tells us not only that *they* do not use it, but that they do not expect *others* to use it.

Clearly, they are not holding anyone accountable.

Clearly, they are not "leading" the charge for performance.

It really is—or ought to be—embarrassing: that it is said, that it is true, that nothing is done about it, that we all accept it.

The press, citizens, interest groups, congressional oversight committees, and citizens should demand more.

"My Managers Aren't Interested"

Well, you know, that's probably not far from the truth. But the real question is, "What are you going to do about it?"

In some ways, you and your managers are tied together. They are a mirror of you.

Would they even dare to show lack of enthusiasm if you had made it clear that performance measures and performance management are important?

Your managers are very busy. Many are managing large and increasing workloads with stable or declining staff and budget resources. Every new administration brings a new set of priorities and programs that must be added to a stable base. Some few catch the updraft of a new program or initiative that has a growing budget.

An investment in performance management without your making it a priority may not seem worth it.

Managers may feel that they already have a pretty good sense of what their program is doing. If they have been connected to a program for some period of time, they have many ways of staying on top of management, policy, and political issues.

One can wish they would be more proactive in relation to performance management, adhere to a higher sense of public service (GPRA is the law), and be more aware of the importance of a performance orientation in today's world.

But in the last analysis, the buck stops at your desk. If you said it was important, they would do it.

Sorry, there's no other way to say it.

And, you know, a few moments of reflection would undoubtedly lead you to conclude that performance-based management ought to be among your top priorities. Truly, when you reflect on your service in the government, how can you not ask what you stand for? What level of public service, professionalism, citizenship?

It is a well-known fact in Washington that many career managers are not going full out in support of performance-based management.

And everybody knows why.

Recommended Responses

1. Learn about performance-based management. Ask someone to pull together some reading for you. There's plenty of it. Find out what's happening around the world and why. Performance-based management is being driven by important economic, social, and technical forces that are reshaping world economics and politics. You need to know.

2. Set an example somewhere. Start with a program of special interest to you. Think it through. Seek expert advice. Ask the questions: How can the highest level of performance in this program be achieved? What would be the best way to articulate its goals, define its objectives, and measure its performance? Talk about what you are learning, the decisions you are making, and the results you are getting. And it won't be long before some of your senior managers are telling you their experiences as well.

"It's Not Useful to Me"

This is truly a stunning statement.

It is all the more stunning because it is expressed at the highest levels among political appointees—not on formal occasions, but on enough informal ones that the message gets around.

Some of this is understandable. Let's make the case as well as we can:

- Top-level officials spend more time on politics and policy than management.
- The Government Performance and Results Act, the legal framework requiring performance measures, belonged to the Clinton administration.
- The President's Management Agenda belongs to the Bush administration.

Now let's make the case as it should be made:

- Top-level officials may spend more time on politics and policy, but they are also responsible for management.
- The Government Performance and Results Act is the law.
- The President's Management Agenda is so closely interwoven with the Government Performance and Results Act that the two cannot be separated. GPRA is the legal and management framework for the PMA.

And OMB's new budget process based on the Program Assessment Rating Tool uses the budget process to drive GPRA objectives, including performance measures, deep into the heart of management.

So the statement—"It's not useful to me"—reveals, at best, an incomplete understanding of the "utility" of performance information in today's management context.

But the statement is more important for what it reveals about both the state of the art in agencies and the attitude of agency leaders.

It is entirely possible that indicators and measures are not useful to top political appointees. The process of developing, installing, and using performance information is new. Top leaders of both parties have not been deeply involved in the process, instead relegating the task to subordinates, special assistants, and particular offices. If GPRA plans and reports look like paperwork, that's because they were often treated that way. In some agencies, the leader has never read any of the performance planning or reporting documents.

Performance information should be useful to political leaders. It should be among the most useful capacities they have for managing resources and communicating value to citizens. Having clear goals, objectives, and performance indicators ought to be a number one priority.

Recommended Responses

1. Top political leaders should be leading the charge to develop and use performance information. They are stewards of the public resources. They are here in Washington on behalf of their fellow citizens. This is a fundamental responsibility.

2. If, as sometimes is the case, a performance management information system does not yield information needed by a cabinet secretary or other official, either because it is not fully developed or because it does not have a specific piece of information needed in a given context, the system should be supplemented with an in-place capacity to provide the needed information.

   In short, if Congress calls, there needs to be a capacity to answer. No system will ever anticipate all eventualities. That is not a fault of the system, which cannot be all things to all people. But the system can and should be supplemented with an in-place staff capacity to provide information on an ad hoc basis through such methods as survey research, interviews, case studies, and analysis of existing data systems. Such a capacity should be directly available to those in need and able to respond within the often-urgent context of the moment. Congress, interest groups, and others have a right to ask questions and get answers.

"Congress Is Not Interested"

This is certainly true enough to be taken very seriously, although not as much as it used to be.

It tells us something important about the Congress.

The GPRA legislation originated in the Senate, where it was sponsored by the late Senator William Roth (R-Del.). There was never a groundswell of support for the bill, but there were a handful of senators and representatives who took an interest. Most of the early support in Congress came from Republicans; Democrats tended to feel it was an attempt to cut programs.

Reports by the Congressional Research Service and others have shown that the number of pieces of legislation and the number of committee reports that make reference to the Government Performance and Results Act are increasing. Occasional committee oversight hearings have been held in both houses of Congress on the Results Act. Some individual Hill staff have supported the idea of performance-based government, and several of them—such as Marcus Peacock and Robert Shea—took positions at OMB and continued to support the evolution of performance-management principles.

But it is certainly true that Congress has shown a modest level of interest. Several years ago at a retreat for congressional staff directors, the agenda included a session on progress under the Government Performance and Results Act. The staff directors in attendance listened and left. They had almost no questions. The few comments made revealed how completely uninterested they were not only in GPRA but in anything having to do with the management of programs in the executive branch.

One is left with the impression that their overriding concern is getting federal dollars to their districts.

The question is: Should this be their only concern? Should they not also be interested in the performance of the executive branch in managing the dollars they appropriate?

The answer has to be yes, even if it is not acknowledged.

And political leaders in the executive branch need to do the right thing and keep the issue of performance in front of the Congress, even when it shows no interest.

Many on the Hill steadfastly cling to the existing budget format not because it is better but because it is familiar and makes it easier for them to track money to their constituents. But these budget formats are as arcane as the agency accounting and organizational systems that produce them, and for exactly the same reason—Congress enacts a program and an agency adds a budget line; the momentum driving both is politics.

There's nothing wrong with politics, but there's nothing wrong with good management and good accounting, either.

Recommended Responses
1. This is one of those issues on which executive branch political leaders should bite the bullet and insist on taking steps to rationalize their budget presentations to Congress despite the anticipation that it will not be welcomed. One strategy is to present two budgets, one in the old format and one in the new, with a crosswalk between them. If this is done year after year, it will become increasingly difficult for congressional staff to argue that they cannot follow money to their favorite programs and districts.
2. Top agency leaders should put themselves on the line by going to the Hill themselves to talk informally with committee members and staff to explain why a performance-oriented format is in the best interests of everyone, including citizens. There is high ground to be claimed. Federal funds belong neither to the Congress nor an agency. Both are trustees for the citizens on whose behalf they serve.

"Citizens Aren't Interested"

This kind of remark is not often heard at high levels among agency political leaders.

But it is surprisingly common at mid levels in situations where political appointees are talking with career civil servants with whom they work on a day-to-day basis.

Often it is made within a context where a close working relationship has evolved and created an atmosphere of colleagueship. Shirtsleeves are rolled up and defenses down.

It is, however, a widespread feeling.

And not without justification.

Citizens are not rising up all over the country and demanding "performance indicators" and "strategic plans." Nor are they calling out for "outcome measures."

It is certainly true that most citizens are not aware of the Government Performance and Results Act.

All that being said, however, it is still surprising to hear the remark made. It is so fundamentally inappropriate.

One might ask: What piece of management improvement legislation do citizens respond to? What should they notice? The average citizen knows little about the day-to-day management of the government. Nor does he or she need to. What do citizens need to know of strategic planning and performance measurement, of program evaluation and financial accounting? Not much.

But they need to be assured that their tax dollars are being managed wisely, and those in the professional public service—whether political or career—must be able to account for their trusteeship.

Those in public service need to have performance measures whether citizens ask for them or not. They need them for themselves, to have a way of monitoring and documenting their activity.

Also, there is ample evidence that while citizens may not be calling for "performance measures" and "strategic plans," they are increasingly interested in results. They want to know that their government has accountability systems in place.

Survey after survey has shown that citizens do not feel their government is as effective or responsive as it could be. They do not look at the federal government as a "high-performing organization." Rightly or wrongly, they see government as being a distant second to private industry in terms of management capacity.

In general, people who work in government, whether political or career, do not think of citizens as often as they should. Probably they are too absorbed in trying to get the day's work done.

But all of them ought to think, talk, and act more within the context of their responsibility to the citizens they serve.

Recommended Responses
1. Study national demographic trends. All public servants should consider and learn more about our nation's citizens. How many are we? Of what age, income level, educational attainment, skill or profession? Where do we live—town or city, poor area or rich? What do we need in terms of social services? It is surprising how many come to Washington and leave having never really thought deeply about the characteristics of the citizen population.
2. Political leaders would do well to develop a specific strategy for communicating to citizens. Many give speeches to a wide range of groups, and so feel that they are making an effort to communicate. In fact, they are speaking to a very small number of very well-defined and organized interests who spend a good deal of time and effort trying to get their attention. Most citizens are quite distant from this kind of communication and know nothing about it.

"It's Hard to Tell …"

"what we're using our performance indicators for," the sentence continues.

This kind of apparently benign estimation, accompanied by a thoughtful moment of silence, speaks volumes about its maker.

How can it be hard to tell if performance information is being used? Is the speaker not a user? Not involved? Not the leader?

Who is responsible? Who makes the decisions?

To some extent, it can be expected that a top political leader will not in fact know the detailed patterns of use within the agency. Agencies are large and complex. They manage hundreds of programs through thousands of people.

But in other aspects, it is hard to understand. If management is important, and performance is important to management, and performance information is important to management, then top leaders will know exactly how it is being used—at least priority management areas.

That a remark as seemingly casual and distant as "it's hard to tell" can be comfortably made seems to suggest that the only place where performance information could be used is "somewhere over there."

If the remark is a prelude to some thoughtful reflection on why managers do and don't take to using performance measures, it might have some welcome legitimacy.

But it is often made in a casual and dismissive way, as if to say, "I don't know too much about that," or "Not a lot of instances of use have come to my attention."

In any case, it raises the fundamental issue of who is leading. Is the leader the leader? What does leadership mean?

At the least, this kind of attitude conveys a very weak sense of commitment, urgency, or priority on the part of the person making it.

Jaded is the word that comes to mind. *Noncommittal* is another.

Recommended Responses
1. In today's world, where performance information is an integral part of an emerging economic climate in which effectiveness and efficiency are at the heart of competition, a casual attitude toward the use of performance information almost guarantees a noncompetitive result. Performance information is not a nice option. It is a fundamental necessity. One way to assure that it receives priority attention is to ask each program manager to prepare an annual plan of use. Such a plan could be very brief but should include a statement about the expected use of priority performance measures.
2. It would not be a bad idea to prepare an annual report on the use of performance information. Such a report would not have to document a one-to-one correspondence between each performance measure and a given decision. Few decisions are made on the basis of performance information alone. But documenting the factors taken into account when a decision is made would have the effect of educating managers and staff on the many ways in which performance (or any other) information is used.

"OMB Is Using the PART"

This is true, although probably not in the way intended.

The intent is to suggest that the Program Assessment Rating Tool process is taking the place of the Results Act.

At higher levels in departments and agencies and among those less familiar with the PART process, GPRA requirements, and what is happening between the two in the current context, it may appear that the PART has replaced GPRA and, therefore, performance measures are no long either required or being emphasized.

Nothing could be further from the truth.

GPRA is law. The PART cannot substitute for law.

And even if the PART could substitute for GPRA, its requirements in relation to performance measures are *more,* not *less,* forceful than those in GPRA.

GPRA requires performance measures as a matter of law. The PART requires performance measures to satisfy the budget process. In other words, if you want money, you need measures.

This is a crude formulation, and no one at OMB would agree to it. But, clearly, OMB is using the PART/budget process to drive performance measurement deep into management processes.

As a part of the PART review, an agency's performance measures are scrutinized and assessed. OMB may find them acceptable or unacceptable. This judgment is recorded in a short report that is issued following each PART analysis.

Moreover, an agency's budget—which under the PART process must include performance measures—becomes that agency's performance plan.

A recent GAO report on the PART process makes the point that the current OMB process is substituting a narrower budget framework (the PART) for a more strategic planning framework (GPRA).

But that is the process today.

Political appointees need to know the law. It is not acceptable public service for a political appointee to ignore the law in furtherance of a politically determined management priority, especially when that politically determined management priority has not been subjected to the scrutiny of national debate.

Recommended Responses

1. Public servants in cognizant management positions, whether career or noncareer, have the same responsibility to execute the law. Those responsible for agency fulfillment of PART and GPRA requirements should fully understand the legal requirements of the latter. GPRA is the law. PART is an OMB management initiative. It is entirely possible

to satisfy PART objectives while at the same time carrying out the legal responsibilities mandated by the Results Act.

2. In clarifying their understanding of the relationship between the PART and GPRA, all who are connected with both should understand that the PART is a budget activity while GPRA has a broader strategic purpose. Therefore, one cannot substitute completely for the other. Each serves a distinct purpose. They need to be maintained as separate documents. They are closely—even intimately—related, but they cannot be the same. Strategy should drive the budget, not vice versa.

"I Never Have What I Need"

This is a remark often made by political leaders and rarely responded to effectively by career civil servants.

In part, this is because the kind of information most urgently needed by political appointees frequently has to do with some current emergency or priority issue that falls outside of the normal management or performance information systems of the agency.

In part, as well, it is because career civil servants—and the information systems they manage—don't focus on these kinds of issues.

Careerists tend to have a longer-range, systems view. They see the application of resources to information systems as a long-term investment. They look back and remember what they consider to be inefficient redirections of long-term system improvements to meet short-term needs, and they look ahead to political leaders yet to come with additional needs.

Their feelings may arise from impelling circumstances, and their intent may be good. But, by and large, they do not give sufficient priority and attention to the short-term information needs of their top leaders.

There is no reason, except lack of will and imagination, for top political leaders not to have a good bit of the information they need, even in circumstances that cannot be fully anticipated. Resource limitations may dictate spending, but they do not curtail the imagination or totally eliminate the capacity.

Some things can and should be anticipated. Political leaders often want information about program funding and activities in congressional districts or certain neighborhoods. Much of the information available on federal funding is available for states, cities, counties, and tribes. But there is no reason why methods cannot be at the ready to estimate funding in other types of jurisdictions. The counter argument is that the government could not run if each party redesigned its information systems by changing the units in which data is collected. True enough. But this is carrying the point to an extreme. There are many things that can be done short of completely redesigning a given system that can help to provide the needed information.

And there are many other contexts in which top political leaders need information that is not tied to congressional districts and which present different kinds of problems: a fire devastates a public housing project, making the evening news, and information is needed about damages and plans for repairing it; a hurricane sweeps up the East Coast, leveling thousands of homes, and questions need to be answered about the effectiveness of remedial aid.

These are performance issues. There may be no cost-effective way to design performance measures to anticipate these kinds of circumstances, but there is no reason why some of the resources assigned to performance measurement cannot be set aside to handle such unanticipated information needs.

It is an accepted tenet of performance-based management that no performance indicator should appear without an accompanying contextual statement providing necessary explanatory information. In other words, context is important. And if it is important in routine performance management, then surely it is appropriate in emergency performance management, and so is fully worthy of attention. In fact, one can argue that there is a continuum of contextual information from routine measurement processes, where a minimum of contextual information is needed, through to non-routine measurement processes, where the performance information needed is almost completely contextual.

Recommended Responses

1. Establish a specific staff capacity or function to handle ad hoc needs for performance information. There are a variety of non-routine situations that require performance information, and they should be recognized as legitimate and provided for. Something should be done. Leaving a cabinet secretary or an assistant secretary too alone, as it sometimes seems, to handle urgent crises, knowing full well that such crises will develop, without making some provision for handling them is just bad public service. Some forethought and effort need to be put into the question of how to satisfy ad hoc performance information needs.
2. Develop specific protocols (methodologies) for adapting information in existing information systems to urgent needs as well as for collecting new information based on samples in very short time periods. These should be in place and ready for emergency needs. Creativity can help. For example, most agencies have field offices around the country. Samples could be predrawn for each field office for each program, and contacts or respondents could be prearranged so that when information is needed, it can be gathered quickly.

"My People Know What I Want"

Very good, if true.

Are you sure?

Who are you thinking of? Your fellow appointees, especially those closest to you?

And why not? You all work for the same president. All came in on the same nickel. All will leave at the same time. All have the same scorecard.

Or, do you?

The general pattern is for top appointees to come in swearing fealty to the boss in the White House but gradually slipping over into at least a partial advocacy position for the groups with a vested interest in the programs of their department. It's only natural. Politics and policies come up against the real world, and there's give and take.

But if you do it, they do it—and the implication of that is that no one under you or around you is totally aligned with your priorities.

Another factor to consider is the very large number of people in your department who actually deliver services where the rubber meets the road—in field offices in local settings all over the country, very distant from you. Experience suggests that for these people—the majority of whom work for you—the coming and going of political administrations (including your own arrival and departure)—have very little impact or meaning. Many are not able to articulate the president's priorities, let alone your own.

It is very easy to forget how large the government is, how hard it is to communicate—let alone effectuate—policies and priorities; and how short a span of time each administration has to pursue its goals.

Performance goals and measures can be a very effective way to communicate your priorities, deploy your resources, and pursue your goals.

It has been said with much truth that what gets measured gets done. Declare a goal and measure, and you have effectively turned on a bright spotlight illuminating all that goes on in your area of interest.

Assuming that your people know what you want and that you have things under control because you are the leader is a very weak reed on which to lean.

Recommended Responses

1. Use some portion of the effort you devote to performance-based management, as required by GPRA and related performance-based administration initiatives, to communicate your top priority interests throughout your organization. Use whatever devices you can afford to spread the message: videotaped speeches by you, videotaped conferences, printed brochures and guidebooks, personal appearances and speeches.

2. Set up a hot line directly to you that employees can use on an anonymous basis to report issues needing to be addressed or to communicate new ideas for improvement. This may be among the most valuable things you can do to achieve your priorities. Much talent and expertise reside in the mid and lower reaches of your organization, and especially outside the beltway. Open up a channel, and you will be able to tap into it. The one inviolable rule is that the channel has to be confidential. The confidentiality of participants must be protected.

"I Already Know ..."

"what I need to know"—is the surprising reaction of some leaders when asked whether they have or rely on performance information, indicators, or measures.

This is an extreme expression of the view that the major job of political leaders is to deal with politics and policy.

According to this view, neither requires great expertise in program operations, including information and analysis relating to program performance.

The custodial functions of public servants, political or career, are simply not taken into account.

To some, it may seem hard to imagine that appointed leaders in high places could see their responsibilities in such narrowly political (and often narrowly partisan) terms.

But for those career public servants who have made public service their profession, this kind of approach is more prevalent than one would expect.

For some, a political appointment is a very, very big step up—from a small position to a big one, from a small town to Washington, from a smaller salary to a larger one, from a place far removed from the corridors of power to the nation's capital. But not for everyone. At the highest levels, those who accept political appointments are frequently giving up substantial executive positions, accepting far lower salaries, and turning their backs on large investment portfolios. Truly, these people make an enormous sacrifice in coming to Washington.

But as one goes down from the top through successive layers of appointees, it is often clear that this situation is reversed.

It is undeniable that for some individuals a political appointment is the capstone of a long career or the cornerstone of a younger one.

The seasoning process for executive talent is no different in the public sector than it is in the private sector. Among other things, a career separates out those who will move higher from those who will not.

This sorting-out process is completely normal. Over the long term of a career cohort, narrower views tend to give way to a broader one, lower to higher, and so on.

But the process itself does have consequences, and they are important—whenever narrower views prevail.

Political appointees, especially younger or less senior ones, would do well to remember that life is, among other things, a report card. There's one on each of us. It tends to be known by our associates. And over the course of a career, it is surprising how the people we meet, even in peripheral circumstances, tend to come in and out of our lives.

You don't come to Washington and leave with a diploma. You come and leave with a record. And that record has an effect on whether you come back again, as well as on successive career steps in the private sector.

Recommended Responses:

1.   Honor the public service and respect public servants. Public service is an honor, and it should be honored by every public servant. One is not in Washington only as a faithful member of a political party but as an American citizen acting in trust for all other citizens. There is no higher secular activity than to serve on behalf of one's neighbors.
2.   Incoming political appointees should read several good biographies of outstanding public servants, people whose lives have made a difference. Not only will this elevate thought, but it will likely sober it as well, for the path to distinction in almost every endeavor, it seems, is 80 percent perspiration, 10 percent inspiration, and 10 percent luck. Don't get caught counting on luck alone.

Communicating Performance Information

A strange transformation occurs after an election, when new political leaders take office.

During the election, the out party is outraged at any lack of disclosure evidenced by the party in office. Every undisclosed detail is fervently seized upon as evidence of ill intent, bad management, or worse.

Disclosure becomes an end in itself, and an almost impossible retrospective standard is established.

Once in office, the incoming administration will rapidly lose interest in this issue and will probably be no better than the last in communicating to the public.

All this is known and expected.

Less well known is that once they are in office, political administrations of both parties do not think very much about "citizens"—about what they should know, about what our democratic political system requires them to know, about communicating information about "performance." They think mainly about carrying out their agenda, successfully negotiating the midterm congressional elections, and preparing the way for a second term.

Something worse happens: They abstract citizens into a broad, amorphous group whose opinions and views need to be managed.

Rarely is there a recognition that there is a responsibility inherent in our political system to fairly, accurately, and promptly communicate to citizens about the administration's performance in relation to the management of their tax dollars.

A higher standard is needed.

"The Public Isn't Interested"

How do you know?

Whom have you talked to lately from "the public"?

In fact, whom have you talked to anywhere about performance information?

Likely, no one from "the public" and maybe no one at all.

To say that the public is not interested in performance information is a little disingenuous. Should they be? What are you there for? Aren't they counting on you?

Let's put the question a little differently.

Is the public interested in performance? I think they are. It's their money we're spending. Do they want to know all of the performance information about government programs? Probably not. Do they want it when they are interested in a particular program? Almost certainly. Do they want to know performance is being watched closely by you and that all the performance information necessary to track the expenditure of public dollars is available and being watched by you? You bet.

The point is that the public, like you and your agency, is learning its way toward performance-based management. There is a set of concepts to be learned, a new vocabulary, and new methods.

But to reduce the issue to its core: Who among the public, what individual citizen, does not want his or her tax dollars spent with due diligence? What citizen would want less than your best effort in managing public resources?

Part of your job in the public service is to communicate what you do. This may require some translation. Few outside of government are experts in its operation and vocabulary. And there is no reason why they should be.

It is your specific responsibility in the public service to act on their behalf, to do what they would want you to do if they were here to do it. It isn't you versus them, you knowledgeable people on the inside versus them out there.

Most people have a high degree of interest in their money and what is done with it, and this is especially true in regard to taxes. Many people work hard for the dollars they give to their government. They want to know that you are working just as hard to spend them wisely.

Recommended Responses
1. Develop a communications strategy designed specifically to communicate to the public. Given likely resource limitations, this will probably mean selecting a limited number of high-priority areas and targeting specific subgroups of citizens. Each program and activity exists within a particular social and economic context. Take some initial steps to see what is most effective. Consider both print and video.
2. Take some portion of your speech-making agenda and target it specifically to the issue of communicating results about a priority program or activity to a specific group of citizens. Use this experience to learn how to use performance information. Apply this experience to subsequent communication activities. Eventually, this will cohere into a useful body of information on communicating to the public, or more properly to different publics.

"It's Not Important ..."

"enough for me to deal with"—is sometimes the response to a question about communicating program activity.

And sometimes the response seems reasonable.

When you're waiting in the outer office of a cabinet secretary while people come and go, some speaking to his or her top administrative assistant, it's easy to sense that the secretary is a very important person. Actually being in the secretary's office, with its lush carpeting, opulent couches and chairs, polished dark-wood paneling, and windows with panoramic views of Washington, you sense that a cabinet secretary is a very high level and important person.

In this setting, the secretary does not seem to be someone who can be expected to be involved in the details of communicating progress in the implementation of performance-based management.

Until we remember that this person was appointed as a part of a political administration whose leader is elected every four years by all the citizens to serve and advance their interests, among which is the wise and prudent use of public funds.

Performance-based management has at its core a focus on services, costs, and quality.

Political appointees have no more fundamental responsibility than to manage the resources entrusted to their care in a responsible and *transparent* manner.

The very best performance management system, one with perfect output and outcome indicators and accurate cost information, has only done half of its job if the information it yields is not effectively communicated to the public.

Good management is half the job; good communication is the other half.

There's a specific reason why this is deeply rooted in our system of government.

We are very proud of the fact that we are a democracy. But a democracy cannot function without information. Citizens cannot wisely vote if they are not well informed.

The political executive who faithfully and competently manages his agency's programs but does not communicate effectively to citizens is not adhering to the highest standards of public service.

Recommended Responses
1. A good first step for a cabinet secretary would be to indicate to all subordinate appointees that communication relative to performance is a priority. This would send a clear signal throughout the agency and begin to provide incentives to the system. While it might be useful to set aside additional resources for this purpose, it is not essential. There are many existing processes, activities, events, and products in every agency that could be utilized. These include training sessions, conference workshops, congressional hearings, speeches, mandated local citizen meetings, and so on. The point is that a signal can be given.
2. All cabinet secretaries have a number of priorities assigned to them by the president and several of their own. In regard to these priorities, performance information should be communicated to citizens in an exemplary fashion. It is a requirement that is higher than loyalty to party; it is a requirement to country. This includes, importantly, reporting both information that shows the agency at its best as well as information that shows room for improvement.

"Our Public/Congressional Relations People Do That"

If they do, you're on the wrong track.

Public relations and congressional relations staff facilitate communication and polish images; they do not (or should not) be the primary message developers.

The substance of what you and your agency do is in your hands and yours alone.

There is a direct line of accountability from you to your top political and career managers. That same line extends outward, through you to the public.

PR and congressional relations staff can help you to deliver the message, but only you can decide its most important content.

For those issues that are of the highest priority to the president and to you, the responsibility for the message and its delivery is yours.

Look at it this way: These functions are not as directly accountable in the political process as you and your subordinate appointees. If you were a citizen, would you want to hear from the highest-level cognizant leader or from the press corps?

This is a substantive management responsibility, not an exercise in political image building.

Many things that you are called on to do as a political appointee are entirely and understandably political in nature.

But the reporting of factual elements relative to the progress of programs and services funded by public tax dollars is not one of them.

Even if the news is bad or counter to the policies of the president, you have an obligation to communicate the essential information fairly and honestly, and, importantly, to place your own personal integrity on the line by taking center stage on the most important issues.

It comes with the territory. You hold a high office, and it requires high standards.

Recommended Responses

1. It seems that few appointees spend much time thinking about the distinction between their political and nonpolitical responsibilities. There are differences. One party can favor a certain type of housing program for poor people. The party's general position is known during a political campaign, and citizens respond with their votes. But progress reports on that approach need to be empirical, not political. Honesty, fairness, and good judgment on behalf of the public interest are the standards for both parties. Appointees should make this clear to their PR and congressional relations functions, and assume direct responsibility for communicating progress against goals for their most important activities.

2. An interesting approach would be to invite key "publics"—interest groups, program beneficiaries, and the press—into the agency on a regular basis for in-depth briefings. Top-level political and career civil servants could be present to answer questions. The meetings could be videotaped and made available for distribution. Of course, briefings are a fairly routine occurrence in Washington. But they have a "staged" quality and are often quite formal. The approach envisioned here would be characterized

by informality. These briefings would place the citizen, rather than the agency, at the helm, allowing the meeting to go wherever it might. Additional agency staff could be called in to answer questions as needed.

"The White House Does That"

There is a widespread tendency on the part of political appointees (actually anyone who has not been around long enough to know differently) to assume that the president and his staff are orchestrating much more than they do.

Partly, this is a natural outgrowth of the enormous sense of mission many bring with them, especially in relation to a first-time appointment. There's a boost to the ego as one tells one's colleagues: "I have a presidential appointment. I'm going to be deputy assistant secretary at...." The same rush of excitement that elevates the new deputy assistant secretary elevates the president even higher.

Partly, it is a sense of responsibility, respect, and/or awe so wide and deep that it imagines an enormous presidential staff, highly organized, setting the nation's course with the precision of a machine—indeed, the largest, most successful such machine on the planet.

And, partly, it is a fear of making a mistake, losing face, or embarrassing the administration.

In practice, the Office of the President consists of a relatively small group of people who manage the president's time in minutes and seconds.

A cabinet officer in good standing and in the spotlight for some reason or other may have only minutes, maybe 15 or 20, with the president, and that no more than several times a month.

The point is that it can be a mistake to simply assume that the White House knows, understands, and is taking action—on anything. And in this the government is no different from the private sector. It would be a mistake to make this assumption in any large organization, period.

The White House is, at one level, a relatively small group of people that operates at a distance far removed from the front lines of agency activities. The same is true within agencies. Cabinet secretaries, simply by virtue of their high position, operate at quite a distance from the front lines.

The point is: Don't assume there is intelligent life above you. There may be. You should be on the lookout for it. You should look for and follow a clearly set direction.

But don't assume the White House does that.

Recommended Responses
1.   When in doubt, prepare to act. If it's important, get ready to do it. Look

around. Ask around. Call someone at OMB if you are in doubt. But don't fail to act or prepare to act under the assumption that the Office of the President will or is likely to act.

2. It wouldn't be a bad idea to use some part of your airtime with OMB or the president to outline your communication plan for the president's and your top priority activities. Both OMB and the Executive Office are always looking for good ways to communicate what the administration is doing. There may be some sensitivity to communicating information that concerns problems, but it can be argued that getting out in front of a potential problem is better than getting caught behind it. In the first instance, you have some ability to control the message; in the second, almost none.

"We Produce Tons of Reports"

This is one of the most commonly heard remarks from political appointees, especially from those for whom such an appointment represents an initial contact with official Washington.

It's often followed by one of these statements:

- "Who reads these things?"
- "These reports are useless."
- "How much do they cost?"
- "Who wrote this thing?"
- "These reports are deadly."
- "What a waste!"
- "Why do we do these things?"

And other such comments, which an initial response may be: "True enough. Many are done poorly."

But the question is why should they be done at all, and the answer to that very important question leads in an entirely different direction.

There are two answers: (1) because they are required by law, and public servants are sworn to faithfully carry out the law, and (2) because it's the right thing to do, as required by our democratic political system.

Almost every major piece of legislation—in other words, almost every program and service—requires the executive branch agency responsible for the expenditure and management of funds to provide an annual (or other similar) report to the Congress on what it has done with the money.

Without a regular flow of information, our political system could not work. A democratic political system requires a regular flow of information from citizens to their government and from government to citizens.

That many of these reports are not done well is, sadly, often true. But it is a sorry, sorry excuse for continuing the tradition.

Many are deadly, mechanical recitations of national aggregate statistics, meaningful to almost no one. Frequently, this is not the fault of the authors, who are often given little direction, meager resources, and no priority.

Annual reports required by law should be produced with the same high sense of responsibility given to other legal requirements, or the law itself and the citizens it protects are demeaned.

Recommended Responses

1. Conduct an agencywide review of annual reporting requirements. Assess the quality of past reports in relation to their intended purpose. Take into account the staff, financial, and other resources available to produce and disseminate the reports. Come up with a plan to do a better job. Probably it will be necessary to prioritize what can be done. Probably resources will be limited. Do something to make things better. Doing nothing is not an acceptable alternative.

2. Focus on one or a small number of reports related to the president's priorities and yours. Focus your personal attention on these. Try to do something that others can emulate. Talk with key stakeholders, including OMB, Congress, interest groups, and citizens. Consider replacing or supplementing the printed report with other communication strategies such as online websites, perhaps including interactive elements. Start on a path of experimentation to see what seems to do the best job.

"We Don't Have the Resources"

Of all the reactions expressed in regard to a query about communicating performance information, this may be one of the most common, untrue, and fatal to effective public service.

There is a certain offhandedness about the way this statement is made.

When, for example, do we ever hear anyone say that he has all the resources he needs? When—I can't recall ever hearing this in a 30-year public service career—do we ever hear anyone say that she has "enough" resources? Or "what is needed to do the job"?

Is it not part of being a smart player to always guard against a possible decrease in funding, to always lay the groundwork for a budget increase, and throughout to portray your activity, program, office, or agency as struggling mightily against heavy odds to delivery important services?

Turning the tables a bit, how often do we hear this comment when the issue is a very high-priority activity? Who wants to be seen as a complainer when the president or a cabinet secretary just wants it done?

The point is that it's easy to say "resources are scarce." The problem is that it's almost always true for almost everything.

And in regard to communicating information about program progress, management initiatives, or service delivery, these words have an especially hollow sound because the legislation and appropriation for many programs provides for an annual report to Congress.

The truth is that neither political nor career public servants give much attention to these requirements. Typically, the agency stays in touch with its appropriations committee, keeping it supplied with whatever information it asks for during the year, and the production of annual reports is a low-priority chore.

A career civil servant assigned to produce an annual report for a non-controversial program in its 10th year of operation can be sure his career is on the skids.

To be sure, more interest is paid to these reports in the early years of new programs or initiatives or when there is some problem or crisis. Otherwise, few care.

The point is that this is a funding source for communicating to the public on performance issues.

Recommended Responses
1. To make the point in a big way, ask someone to list all of the annual reporting requirements and estimate the staff and other costs associated with their production and distribution. It is likely that the magnitude of the resources devoted to this seemingly innocuous task will be compelling. By itself, this will likely alert everyone that the task has to be taken seriously.
2. Ask subordinate bureau and program managers to come up with a communications plan that uses available resources in the most effective way to report fundamental performance information about costs and results to every citizen. The same report can also be used to communicate information on the administration's priority initiatives. *But its first and fundamental obligation is to provide an accurate and faithful accounting for the management of public resources.*

"It's Not That Important"

"It's just not a priority." "I have a lot of things to do." "We do so many things." Or words to this effect.

Writing reports. It seems so innocuous. So inconsequential. So unexciting. To both political and career public servants.

Here are 10 reasons why it needs to be done, and well:
1. Public servants must inform citizens.
2. Public servants must inform citizens.
3. Public servants must inform citizens.

4. Public servants must inform citizens.
5. Public servants must inform citizens.
6. Public servants must inform citizens.
7. Public servants must inform citizens.
8. Public servants must inform citizens.
9. Public servants must inform citizens.
10. Public servants must inform citizens.

Our system of government cannot work effectively unless there is a flow of information from citizens to public servants and from public servants to citizens.

Citizens express their wishes; public servants carry them out.

The system can't work without effective two-way communication.

It helps to remember that public servants are (1) paid by and responsible to citizens, and (2) entrusted with and responsible for the effective management of citizen dollars.

We don't half remember this enough—political and career public servants.

We tend to abstract what we do until we lose sight of our neighbors and friends, no longer seeing them as individuals and citizens, but as "beneficiaries and non-beneficiaries," "eligibles and non-eligibles," "low- or low-to-moderate-income people," and so on.

It's easy to do. No one intends any disrespect.

But we forget.

We need to remember.

Recommended Responses

1. Pick a neighborhood, county, city, or beneficiary group and make it your business to really understand its problems and needs and the way your agency addresses both. It may be a revealing experience with implications far beyond the small ones you have come to know. The point is to put a face on the citizens you serve. It will help you with every other thing you do.

2. Pick a small sample of program beneficiaries and follow them closely. Find out all you can from your program records. Call them directly to express interest and learn more. Call them periodically to see if you can build a useful dialogue. It may be necessary to inform whoever you call that the call is "on the record" and to keep a transcript of the call. But just as a personal visit on the part of a top executive to the desk of a lower-echelon employee can inject a sense of interest and concern, so a call to a program participant or beneficiary can convey a sense of commitment and responsibility. Both are easy to do and can pay dividends. The same can be said of visits to service delivery sites and direct meetings with citizens.

About the Contributors

Mark A. Abramson is Executive Director of the IBM Center for The Business of Government, a position he has held since July 1998. Prior to the Center, he was chairman of Leadership Inc. From 1983 to 1994, Mr. Abramson served as the first president of the Council for Excellence in Government. Previously, Mr. Abramson served as a senior program evaluator in the Office of the Assistant Secretary for Planning and Evaluation, U.S. Department of Health and Human Services.

He is a Fellow of the National Academy of Public Administration. In 1995, he served as president of the National Capital Area Chapter of the American Society for Public Administration. Mr. Abramson has taught at George Mason University and the Federal Executive Institute in Charlottesville, Virginia.

Mr. Abramson is the co-editor of *Transforming Organizations, E-Government 2001, Managing for Results 2002, Innovation, Human Capital 2002, Leaders, E-Government 2003, The Procurement Revolution,* and *New Ways of Doing Business.* He also edited *Memos to the President: Management Advice from the Nation's Top Public Administrators* and *Toward a 21st Century Public Service: Reports from Four Forums.* He is also the co-editor (with Joseph S. Wholey and Christopher Bellavita) of *Performance and Credibility: Developing Excellence in Public and Nonprofit Organizations,* and the author of *The Federal Funding of Social Knowledge Production and Application.*

He received his Bachelor of Arts degree from Florida State University. He received a Master of Arts degree in history from New York University and a Master of Arts degree in political science from the Maxwell School of Citizenship and Public Affairs, Syracuse University.

Joseph A. Ferrara is Director of the Master of Policy Management program at the Georgetown Public Policy Institute at Georgetown University. At Georgetown, he teaches courses on public management and public policy. Previously he served as a career member of the Senior Executive Service in the U.S. federal government, where he held positions with the House of Representatives, the Office of Management and Budget, and the Department of Defense.

Dr. Ferrara received his B.A. degree from the College of Charleston, his M.P.A. from the University of South Carolina, and his Ph.D. from Georgetown University.

Dana Michael Harsell is an Assistant Professor at Hartwick College, in Oneonta, New York, where he teaches classes in American government, public administration, and political psychology. His research interests include administrative state reform, public management, and managing for results. While at the Maxwell School of Syracuse University, Professor Harsell worked as a research assistant for the Government Performance Project and helped assess the managing-for-results capacity of 40 of the nation's largest county governments. He also spent a year as the project manager for the New Jersey Initiative, which used Government Performance Project methodology to assess the management capacities of municipal-level governments in New Jersey.

Professor Harsell holds a B.A. in political science and psychology and an M.A. in political science, both from the University of Montana, and is near completion of a Ph.D. in political science from Syracuse University. Upcoming publications include a chapter in *Managing for Performance in State and Local Government,* edited by Patricia Ingraham, and an article in the *Journal of Political Science Education.*

Dr. Paul R. Lawrence is a Partner with IBM's Business Consulting Services. He works with federal executives, helping them solve complex problems by applying solutions proven in similar government settings or the private sector.

Dr. Lawrence is also the Partner-in-Charge of the IBM Center for The Business of Government (www.businessofgovernment.org), which seeks to advance knowledge on how to improve public sector effectiveness. He hosts the weekly radio show, "The Business of Government Hour," heard on WJFK-FM 106.7 Saturdays, 9–10 a.m., where he interviews government leaders about their job, career, and vision for the future of government. Since the show began in 1999, he has interviewed 150 senior government leaders in the Clinton and Bush administrations. He is the editor of *The Business of Government Journal.* He is also the co-editor of *Transforming Organizations* and the editor of the IBM Center for The Business of Government book series, which has produced 15 books on government management topics (www.rowmanlittlefield.com/series).

Dr. Lawrence has written extensively on technology and government and has testified before Congress and several state legislatures. He serves on the Board of Advisors of the Thomas Jefferson Public Policy Program at William and Mary and on the Washington, D.C. area Board of Directors of Junior Achievement. He was the chairman of the Board of Directors of the Private Sector Council and was a member of the Advisory Committee to the Virginia Assembly's Joint Committee on Technology and Science. He was twice selected by *Federal Computer Week* as one of the top 100 public service business leaders—in 2000 and in 2002.

Dr. Lawrence graduated Phi Beta Kappa from the University of Massachusetts, with a B.A. in economics. He earned his M.A. and Ph.D. in economics from Virginia Tech.

Judith Michaels is the author of *The President's Call: Executive Leadership from FDR to George Bush.* She is currently a freelance writer and consultant. Dr. Michaels recently conducted the interviews for the *2004 Prune Book: Top Management Challenges for Political Appointees* prepared by the Council for Excellence in Government. She has also served as an adjunct professor in public policy at the Institute for Experiential Learning, in urban policy at Goucher College, and in government and policy at George Mason University. She received a doctoral fellowship at the General Accounting Office, where she developed, administered, and analyzed a survey of Senate-confirmed presidential appointees.

Her degrees include her Ph.D. from the College of Urban Affairs and Public Policy at the University of Delaware, and her Master of Public Administration from the Department of Public Administration, University of Baltimore.

Lynn C. Ross is a Ph.D. candidate in American government at Georgetown University. She is currently working on her dissertation. Her academic interests are in the bureaucracy, the presidency, presidential electoral politics, and budgetary politics.

Before returning to graduate school in 1999, she worked for the U.S. federal government for almost 15 years. Most recently she served as a program examiner in the Executive Office of the President at the Office of Management and Budget. She started her federal career as a Presidential Management Intern in the U.S. Office of Personnel Management.

Ross holds a B.A. degree from the State University of New York at Binghamton and an M.P.A. from the Maxwell School of Citizenship and Public Affairs at Syracuse University.

John H. Trattner is Senior Writer and Editor at the Council for Excellence in Government.

Mr. Trattner is the author of the seven volumes to date in the Council's *Prune Book* series as well as *A Survivors' Guide for Government Executives* and other publications. He served as a career U.S. diplomat for 20 years, with assignments in Warsaw, Strasbourg, Paris, Brussels, and Washington. At the Department of State, he was executive assistant to then deputy secretary of state Warren Christopher and press spokesman of the department under Edmund Muskie. On leaving government in 1983, he served as press secretary to former U.S. Senator George J. Mitchell.

Chris Wye served as Director of the Center for Improving Government Performance at the National Academy of Public Administration from 1994 until 2003. The Center provides assistance to government agencies on improving management processes using the techniques of performance-based management, including strategic planning, performance measurement, program evaluation, performance-based budgeting, and strategic management.

Dr. Wye also was the Director of the Performance Consortium, an organization of 30 federal agency functions that have come together under the Academy's leadership to provide a program of peer-to-peer dialogue, forums, workshops, and conferences to support the exchange of helpful practices related to performance-based management.

Prior to his work with the Academy, Wye spent 20 years in the federal government, directing policy analysis, program evaluation, and program monitoring functions. He has written and published widely on practical, low-cost techniques for improving government performance.

Wye graduated from Parsons College with a B.A. in 1966, and from Kent State University with an M.A. in 1967 and a Ph.D. in 1974.

About the IBM Center for
The Business of Government

Through research stipends and events, the IBM Center for The Business of Government stimulates research and facilitates discussion of new approaches to improving the effectiveness of government at the federal, state, local, and international levels.

The Center is one of the ways that IBM Business Consulting Services seeks to advance knowledge on how to improve public sector effectiveness. The IBM Center focuses on the future of the operation and management of the public sector.

Research stipends of $15,000 are awarded competitively to outstanding scholars in academic and nonprofit institutions across the United States. Each award winner is expected to produce a 30- to 40-page research report in one of the areas presented on pages 207–210. Reports will be published and disseminated by the Center.

Research Stipend Guidelines

Who is Eligible?
Individuals working in:
- Universities
- Nonprofit organizations
- Journalism

Description of Research Stipends
Individuals receiving research stipends will be responsible for producing a 30- to 40-page research report in one of the areas presented on pages

207–210. The report will be published and disseminated by the IBM Center for The Business of Government. The manuscript must be submitted no later than six months after the start of the project. Recipients will select the start and end dates of their research project. The reports should be written for government leaders and should provide practical knowledge and insights.

Size of Research Stipends
$15,000 for each research paper

Who Receives the Research Stipends?
Unless otherwise requested, individuals will receive the research stipends.

Application Process
Interested individuals should submit:
- A three-page description of the proposed research—(please include a 100-word executive summary describing the proposed project's: (a) purpose, (b) methodology, and (c) results)
- A résumé (no more than three pages)

Application Deadlines
There will be two funding cycles annually, with deadlines of:
- March 1
- November 1
  Applicants will be informed of a decision regarding their proposal no later than eight weeks after the deadlines. Applications must be received online or postmarked by the above dates.

Submitting Applications
Online:
businessofgovernment.org/apply
Hard Copy:
Mark A. Abramson
Executive Director
IBM Center for The Business of Government
1301 K Street, NW
Fourth Floor, West Tower
Washington, DC 20005

Research Areas

Research Area One: Changing Rules

Reforming Human Capital

Modernizing Human Resource Management in the Federal Government: The IRS Model by James R. Thompson and Hal G. Rainey (April 2003)

Human Capital Reform: 21st Century Requirements for the United States Agency for International Development by Anthony C. E. Quainton and Amanda M. Fulmer (March 2003)

A Weapon in the War for Talent: Using Special Authorities to Recruit Crucial Personnel by Hal G. Rainey (December 2001)

Improving Financial Management

An Introduction to Financial Risk Management in Government by Richard J. Buttimer, Jr. (August 2001)

Audited Financial Statements: Getting and Sustaining "Clean" Opinions by Douglas A. Brook (July 2001)

Using Activity-Based Costing to Manage More Effectively by Michael H. Granof, David E. Platt, and Igor Vaysman (January 2000)

Focusing on Organizational Reforms

Moving Toward More Capable Government: A Guide to Organizational Design by Thomas H. Stanton (June 2002)

The President's Management Council: An Important Management Innovation by Margaret L. Yao (December 2000)

Transforming Procurement Rules and Practices

Making Performance-Based Contracting Perform: What the Federal Government Can Learn from State and Local Governments by Lawrence L. Martin (November 2002, 2nd ed.)

A Vision of the Government as a World-Class Buyer: Major Procurement Issues for the Coming Decade by Jacques S. Gansler (January 2002)

Managing for Outcomes: Milestone Contracting in Oklahoma by Peter Frumkin (January 2001)

Research Area Two: Emphasizing Performance

Hov Federal Programs Use Outcome Information: Opportunities for Federal Ma igers by Harry P. Hatry, Elaine Morley, Shelli B. Rossman, and Joseph S. Wh ley (February 2004, 2nd ed.)

Li ing Performance and Budgeting: Opportunities in the Federal Budget P cess by Philip G. Joyce (January 2004, 2nd ed.)

rategies for Using State Information: Measuring and Improving Program erformance by Shelley H. Metzenbaum (December 2003)

The Baltimore CitiStat Program: Performance and Accountability by Lenneal J. Henderson (May 2003)

Performance Management for Career Executives: A "Start Where You Are, Use What You Have" Guide by Chris Wye (September 2004, 2nd ed.)

Moving Toward More Capable Government: A Guide to Organizational Design by Thomas H. Stanton (June 2002)

The Challenge of Developing Cross-Agency Measures: A Case Study of the Office of National Drug Control Policy by Patrick J. Murphy and John Carnevale (August 2001)

Using Performance Data for Accountability: The New York City Police Department's CompStat Model of Police Management by Paul E. O'Connell (August 2001)

Research Area Three: Improving Service Delivery

Delivering Services through the Internet

The State of Federal Websites: The Pursuit of Excellence by Genie N. L. Stowers (August 2002)

State Web Portals: Delivering and Financing E-Servicing by Diana Burley Gant, Jon P. Gant, and Craig L. Johnson (January 2002)

The Use of the Internet in Government Service Delivery by Steven Cohen and William Eimicke (February 2001)

Delivering Services through Non-Traditional Organizations

Implementing State Contracts for Social Services: An Assessment of the Kansas Experience by Jocelyn M. Johnston and Barbara S. Romzek (May 2000)

Business Improvement Districts and Innovative Service Delivery by Jerry Mitchell (November 1999)

Religious Organizations, Anti-Poverty Relief, and Charitable Choice: A Feasibility Study of Faith-Based Welfare Reform in Mississippi by John P. Bartkowski and Helen A. Regis (November 1999)

Improving the Internal Operations of Government

Franchise Funds in the Federal Government: Ending the Monopoly in Service Provision by John J. Callahan (February 2002)

Entrepreneurial Government: Bureaucrats as Businesspeople by Anne Laurent (May 2000)

Delivering Government Functions through Market-Based Approaches

Rethinking U.S. Environmental Protection Policy: Management Challenges for a New Administration by Dennis A. Rondinelli (November 2000)

An Assessment of Brownfield Redevelopment Policies: The Michigan Experience by Richard C. Hula (November 1999)

New Tools for Improving Government Regulation: An Assessment of Emissions Trading and Other Market-Based Regulatory Tools by Gary C. Bryner (October 1999)

Research Area Four: Increasing Collaboration

Communities of Practice: A New Tool for Government Managers by William M. Snyder and Xavier de Souza Briggs (November 2003)

The Challenge of Coordinating "Big Science" by W. Henry Lambright (July 2003)

Public-Private Strategic Partnerships: The U.S. Postal Service-Federal Express Alliance by Oded Shenkar (May 2003)

Assessing Partnerships: New Forms of Collaboration by Robert Klitgaard and Gregory F. Treverton (March 2003)

Leveraging Networks: A Guide for Public Managers Working across Organizations by Robert Agranoff (March 2003)

Extraordinary Results on National Goals: Networks and Partnerships in the Bureau of Primary Health Care's 100%/0 Campaign by John Scanlon (March 2003)

21st-Century Government and the Challenge of Homeland Defense by Elaine C. Kamarck (June 2002)

Leveraging Networks to Meet National Goals: FEMA and the Safe Construction Networks by William L. Waugh, Jr. (March 2002)

For more information about the Center

Visit our website at: www.businessofgovernment.org
Send an e-mail to: businessofgovernment@us.ibm.com
Call: (202) 515-4504